Praise for Adam Kahane's Work

Business

"Kahane addresses an important challenge that we face every day: how can we move forward together in situations where we are in conflict and unable to construct a shared vision of the future? In doing this he overturns conventional practice—including his own—and proposes a new approach to collaboration that is better suited to our difficult current context."
—**Jan Kees Vis, Global Director, Sustainable Sourcing Development, Unilever**

"Adam's *Solving Tough Problems* helped me understand that all our pressing problems—be they strategic issues inside a company or societal challenges like conflict, poverty, or climate change—require that those with a stake and the power to act come together in open dialogue to create a joint diagnosis and a deep commitment to moving forward together. In *Power and Love*, Adam goes further and deeper—into the kind of leadership that it takes to do this. A must-read for every reflective leader."
—**Ravi Venkatesan, Director, Infosys, and former Chairman, Microsoft India**

"Our societies face really hard problems—poverty, injustice, unsustainability, corruption—that are insoluble by conventional means. Conflicts of interest and profound uncertainties about the future are producing paralysis and inaction. Adam Kahane has, more than anyone, developed and successfully employed tools that enable us to create futures of shared progress and profit."
—**Peter Schwartz, Senior Vice President, Salesforce.com, and author of *The Art of the Long View***

Civil Society

"In *Collaborating with the Enemy*, Adam Kahane shows that people who don't see eye-to-eye really can come together to solve big challenges. Whether in our businesses, our governments, our communities, or our personal lives, we can all benefit from this smart and timely book."
—**Mark Tercek, President, The Nature Conservancy; former Managing Director, Goldman Sachs; and coauthor of *Nature's Fortune***

"Adam Kahane proposes a solid and clear methodology, supported by his experience in the many processes in which he has participated, that invites us to defy our situation and to transform—not only to change—it, beginning by transforming ourselves."
—**Luis Raúl González Pérez, President, National Human Rights Commission, Mexico**

"Kahane takes the core message from his seminal *Power and Love* into uncharted territory: our messy, challenging, and necessary task of working with others to solve intractable problems. He redefines collaboration, testing our assumptions about the interplay between individual agency and collective action. At once theory, memoir, and practical guide, *Collaborating with the Enemy* is a vital primer for people working at all scales to make the world a better place."
—**Ross McMillan, President, Tides Canada**

"Nowadays, opposition and conflict are the new normal, yet normal responses to them seem impotent. Amid this chaos and as if delivered to us by 'special order,' *Collaborating with the Enemy* shows us how thinking and seeing differently can help us navigate this challenging landscape. Kahane abandons orthodoxy in taking on the most intransigent problems, showing us the path to effective action in a complex world."
—**James Gimian, Publisher, *Mindful* magazine, and coauthor of *The Art of War* and *The Rules of Victory***

"*Transformative Scenario Planning* is a deeply human book that offers tangible means for tackling the intractable problems that confront us at every level of life, from domestic and local to national and beyond. It offers realistic, grounded hope of genuine transformation, and its insights and lessons should be part of the toolbox of everyone in leadership roles."
—**Thabo Makgoba, Anglican Archbishop of Cape Town**

"In our field, the hardest nut to crack is how to address conflicts between parties with fundamentally different worldviews. Adam offers a robust theory and a straightforward practice to address this vital challenge."
—**Ofer Zalzberg, Senior Middle East Analyst, International Crisis Group**

Foundations

"How many of us have dreamed of developing the art of helping others solve 'impossible' problems and bridge 'uncrossable' divides? Adam Kahane has taken that journey. Read, listen, absorb, and integrate."
—Peter Goldmark, former President, The Rockefeller Foundation

"To transcend the perilous state in which we find ourselves, we need to learn to collaborate with those with whom we'd rather not. Drawing on his experience enabling sworn enemies to create peace in places like South Africa, Northern Ireland, and Colombia, Adam Kahane shares insights and lessons we can all use when collaborating with 'those others' is our only or best way forward. *Collaborating with the Enemy* belongs on the same shelf as Sun Tzu's *The Art of War* and Machiavelli's *The Prince*."
—Stephen Huddart, President, The J. W. McConnell Family Foundation

"Adam Kahane helps us overcome romantic and linear approaches to conflict transformation. *Collaborating with the Enemy* provides a hands-on critique of the myth of the uninvolved mediator and explains the art of working with the enemy."
—Gorka Espiau, Associate Director, The Young Foundation, and former Peace Advisor to the President, Basque Government

Government

"Mahatma Gandhi said, 'Be the change you want to see in the world.' His life was the unfolding of an even deeper truth: the need to change himself if he wanted to change the world. Hence, his autobiography was titled *My Experiments with Truth*. Adam's story of his engagements with people in many countries, whom he was called to help in their efforts to change their worlds, is an account of his own realization of Gandhi's deeper insight. It is an honest and beautifully told story."
—Arun Maira, former member, National Planning Commission, and former Chairman, Boston Consulting Group, India

"*Power and Love* includes the story of the Visión Guatemala team, in which a group of us, who in the ordinary course of events would never have met or worked together, had an unprecedented experience that opened up new horizons for us and for our country. Adam helped us cultivate our dreams and ideals and gave us the energy and hope

to act to renew our society."
—**Raquel Zelaya, former Secretary of Peace, Guatemala**

"Advances and changes in humankind have left the world with super-complex problems—from achieving sustainable development to maintaining peace and security—that require changes in the way we face them. *Collaborating with the Enemy* gives us not only a privileged look into Adam's extensive experiences in high-level engagements to address these problems but also his honest and brave reflection on his successes and failures, and from these his articulation of an important new approach to collaboration."
—**Kuntoro Mangkusubroto, former Head, President of Indonesia's Delivery Unit, and Distinguished Practitioner, Blavatnik School of Government, University of Oxford**

"The quality of a decision depends in large part on the quality of the process by which the decision is made. But the political process in my country (as in most) actually causes us to 'enemyfy' each other. If we are to solve the great challenges of our time, whether climate change or economic division and social unravelling, we must learn how to collaborate with those we believe to be our enemies. Adam shows us a way to do so."
—**James Shaw, Member of Parliament and Coleader, Green Party of Aotearoa New Zealand**

Academia

"*Collaborating with the Enemy* is a lighthouse for our troubled times. If we are to find a way to reconcile the divides that imperil our common life, here we have a profound guide and a source of hope."
—**Rufus Black, Master, Ormond College, The University of Melbourne**

"*Power and Love* is a rare and valuable book. Kahane has immersed himself in the practical challenges of helping people effect social change, and against this backdrop he unfolds a simple and penetrating insight: that power and love are two axes that delineate our individual and collective journeys. Either we master the balance of power and love or we will fail in our efforts to realize deep and lasting change."
—**Peter Senge, Senior Lecturer, Massachusetts Institute of Technology, and author of *The Fifth Discipline***

COLLABORATING WITH THE ENEMY

OTHER BOOKS BY ADAM KAHANE

Solving Tough Problems: An Open Way of Talking, Listening, and Creating New Realities

Power and Love: A Theory and Practice of Social Change

Transformative Scenario Planning: Working Together to Change the Future

Collaborating with the Enemy

How to Work with People You Don't Agree with or Like or Trust

Adam Kahane

Drawings by Jeff Barnum

A Reos Partners Publication

BK®

Berrett–Koehler Publishers, Inc.
a BK Business book

BERRETT-KOEHLER PUBLISHERS, INC.
1333 Broadway, Suite 1000, Oakland, CA 94612-1921
Tel: (510) 817-2277   Fax: (510) 817-2278   www.bkconnection.com

ORDERING INFORMATION
Quantity Sales. Special discounts are available on quantity purchases by corporations, associations, and others. For details, contact the "Special Sales Department" at the Berrett-Koehler address above.
Individual Sales. Berrett-Koehler publications are available through most bookstores. They can also be ordered directly from Berrett-Koehler:
Tel: (800) 929-2929; Fax: (802) 864-7626; www.bkconnection.com
Orders for College Textbook/Course Adoption Use. Please contact Berrett-Koehler: Tel: (800) 929-2929; Fax: (802) 864-7626.

Dsitributed to the U.S. trade and internationally by Penguin Random House Publisher Services.

Berrett-Koehler and the BK logo are registered trademarks of Berrett-Koehler, Inc.

PRINTED IN THE UNITED STATES OF AMERICA

Berrett-Koehler books are printed on long-lasting acid-free paper. When it is available, we choose paper that has been manufactured by environmentally responsible processes. These may include using trees grown in sustainable forests, incorporating recycled paper, minimizing chlorine in bleaching, or recycling the energy produced at the paper mill.

Library of Congress Cataloging-in-Publication Data
Names: Kahane, Adam, author.
Title: Collaborating with the enemy : how to work with people you don't agree with or like or trust / Adam Kahane.
Description: First Edition. | Oakland, CA : Berrett-Koehler Publishers, Inc., [2017] | "A Reos Partners Publication." | Includes bibliographical references and index.
Identifiers: LCCN 2016059030 | ISBN 9781626568228 (pbk.)
Subjects: LCSH: Communication in management. | Management—Social aspects. | Conflict management.
Classification: LCC HD30.3 .K34 2017 | DDC 650.1/3—dc23
LC record available at https://lccn.loc.gov/2016059030

FIRST EDITION
22 21 20   10 9 8 7 6 5

Text design: Gopa & Ted2 Design
Cover design: Dan Tesser, Studio Carnelian
Cover art: Shutterstock by Siberia Video and Photo
Edit: Elissa Rabellino
Proofread: Karen Hill Green
Index: Paula C. Durbin-Westby
Production: Linda Jupiter Productions

To my enemies and teachers

Contents

Foreword by Peter Block

*I*f you are working to make the world a better place, there are few experiences more rewarding and useful than having your thinking turned upside down. A shift in thinking is the essence of transformation. It is the basis of renewed faith. It is at the core of great leadership. In most cases the shift happens slowly, perhaps from education or trying to make sense of unsettling experiences, usually occurring without our being aware of it. Once in a while, however, we get lucky. Our mind shifts by simply reading a book. Adam Kahane's *Collaborating with the Enemy: How to Work with People You Don't Agree with or Like or Trust* is such a book.

The book is really an annotation on the title. The title asks me to collaborate with people I don't agree with. Not so difficult. But then the stakes are raised, and I am asked to collaborate with people I don't like. This too is manageable, even common in most workplaces. The final ask, though, is tougher: collaborate with people I don't trust. Even people I consider enemies. To make these acts doable is the promise of the book.

This promise is particularly relevant in light of what is occurring in the world. We live in a complicated time. It is a divisive and polarizing era in which we respond by constantly seeking like-mindedness. We have a growing number of ways to meet up with people similar to ourselves: We are drawn to people with the same interests, same tastes, same politics. Every time I buy something online, I am told what other people like me also bought. And it works. As a larger society, cities are resegregating into neighborhoods of people like us. As nations, we are voting for politicians who want to keep out strangers and reclaim our country as if someone had taken it away.

We live in a time of growing alienation and isolation. We are losing trust in our institutions and our governments to act in our interests. Most of our elections are variations of a "no" vote. We have growing economic divisions, ideological divisions, contests over values.

All this is why Adam's book is important. It offers a way of thinking and action that can create what seems like an impossible future by inviting all sides of a question into one room, *especially* when they don't agree with, like, or trust each other. It describes this way of being and working and does it in a way to make the process accessible. What is also compelling is that Adam and his colleagues have actually put their thinking into practice. The world has been changed by their efforts.

Here are some of the elements of *Collaborating with the Enemy* that have shifted my thinking:

- I have believed that collaborating with others is our first choice. My view has been that human beings are basically collaborative, wanting to work together, and that we just need to remove the obstacles that prevent this from happening. Not so. Collaboration as presented in this book is simply one of several first choices. It is just as likely that our first choice is imposing our point of view on others, forcing compliance when possible, and doing all we can to get our way. Another first choice is to adapt to the world. Make compromises, minimize differences, and go along to get along.

  What Adam describes are ways to think about collaboration when the situation is increasingly hopeless. When we have reached a moment in which trying to control outcomes and impose our position on others is not working. Or, when adapting to the difficulty becomes untenable. The collaboration described here is aimed at finding a new way to move when the current reality is dire, and there is agreement on only one thing: something needs to change. This approach applies—whether for us as individuals, or an organization, or a community—whenever we are forced or ready to try something really new.

- For much of my career I made a living as a consultant to organizations, whether they were businesses, schools, governments, churches, or associations. Much of the work involved helping teams to work better, helping labor and management to build trust with each other, or helping departments within a company to cooperate more effectively. In all these situations it was assumed that people were working toward a common goal. In my perspective, if they did not have a desire and instinct to work together and to trust each other, what was the point of coming together? Adam's basic point is that this is exactly the time to come together.

- As a culture, we believe that the answer to fragmentation and polarization is to develop coalitions and strategies to defeat or weaken the other side. We campaign to prove the superiority of our position. If we are oil companies, tobacco companies, or pharmaceutical companies, we establish so-called independent think tanks to gather research that casts doubt on those who oppose us.

When facing a complex challenge, where prior efforts to achieve results have essentially failed, we invest in a cocktail of marketing strategies, build movements, and mobilize political will to produce the change we desire. In the public arena, the most visible strategies have been the war on drugs, the war on poverty, the war on terrorism, and civil war. We convene summits that craft a declaration and leave us with a set of action steps and a news release. The call to the summit is always to do something for the good of the whole. In times of crisis in the management and organizational world, whenever disruption occurs—a product loses its market or an industry or business is losing its legitimacy to operate—

our propensity is to work at change management. We design culture-shifting programs, initiate training programs, set new standards, find new people, call for more agility and more innovation.

All these are well-accepted strategies and have a net positive impact. They certainly deliver improvements, but most of these transformation efforts are thinly veiled versions of how we try to get other people to change, to shift either their thinking or their actions in alignment with our intention. Colonial in nature, disappointing much of the time.

Where change is stubborn, the conventional strategies suffer from a kind of naïveté. They are constructed on two premises:

One premise is that there is an elite circle of people who know what is best for others and the world. We hold the almost sacred opinion that it is the right and duty of the central circle of leaders and experts to create think tanks; declare war on popular negatives like drugs, poverty, and terror; and select the people who speak and negotiate at the summits. Inside organizations, we basically believe that the central circle is top management and—whether in business, education, the church, or government —they are best equipped to launch the change programs.

The second premise is the belief that we can problem-solve our way into the future. It is a deeply held belief that change will occur when we agree on a vision, set goals and define a predictable path to reach them, and specify observable measures, with timelines and milestones. The glue for all this is our belief and language about holding people accountable and demanding consequences for failure.

Collaborating with the Enemy calls this rational ordering of action into question, especially in the face of complex problems where there are very divergent views and conflicts among important stakeholders. This condition of complex problems, whether in a society or in an organization, calls for a different way. This is where Adam offers something unique.

He talks of stretch collaboration as an alternative to the dominant thinking about how progress is achieved. He outlines a process whereby those who have a long history of distrust, incompatible goals, and embedded stories of not liking each other can create an alternative future without reaching major agreements. This means bringing people with divergent intentions into a room together where the task is not to negotiate or develop action steps. They only need to agree that a condition needs to change, but at no point are they asked to give up their own solutions or story of their position.

A final piece of conventional practice, one that I have held dear and that Adam sets limits on, is that we primarily need to focus on the nature of the conversations between opposing parties and interests. The common paths are to seek understanding through better listening, through carefully structured forms of dialogue, through managing difficult conversations and getting to yes. These methods are always useful, but in the "stretch" approach to collaboration, dialogue is not the main concern. Changing the conversation as the primary means of creating an alternative future is not enough. Something more is called for.

This stretch collaboration has three major tenets, which I will only name here. You need to read the book to do them justice. First, we have to affirm the legitimacy and value of every stance and each of its advocates. This idea manifests the belief that there is more than one worldview or mind-set to be considered. It reflects the thinking in a statement often attributed to Niels Bohr: "For every great idea, the opposite idea is also true."

Second, the way forward in the form of collaboration Adam describes is through experientially learning together. We set aside any effort at coming up with negotiated certainties and engage in joint experimentation. Everyone has an opinion, and it is only by trying some things together that we can jointly see which ones will work in the situation at hand.

Finally, Adam calls us to place attention on the consciousness of ourselves and the people working to achieve collaboration.

This is for anyone in the position of trying to bring enemies together. This consciousness is to be present in a new way, one in which we are able to notice what is occurring in the world rather than trying to impact it. And to notice that we are as much a player in the moment as anyone else in the room.

In addition to the ideas it presents, the book is important because it is written with humility and an acceptance of our humanity. Adam talks about how his own attempts to force collaboration have in fact worked to prevent it. He supports the theory with very concrete examples of how people have found ways to honor and acknowledge the legitimacy of their enemies and create futures that once seemed impossible. The book is insightful as much for its stories as for its theory.

Underlying the book is an unnamed spiritual dimension. It uses the language of Power and Love, the title of another of Adam's books. This language evokes aspects of collaboration that hold a place for mystery. For things unknowable, impossible to define. Collaboration of this kind arises in certain moments in the life of a group that shift the context of the effort and open the possibility of something new occurring. This is most likely to happen when there is recognition of our equal capacity to exercise power and to love, both at the same time, with the same people.

What comes through in the book is a call for wholeness. It asks us to face the harsh reality of the political and human suffering in the world, the existence of seemingly un-negotiable conflicts, long histories of contempt. At the same time, it invites us to include in our thinking the possibility of enemies having a useful place in our longing for a different future. Also, to do this work we have to inquire into ourselves, individually, as conscious, learning, and mistake-making human beings; we have to accept that, in the face of our good will, we can lose trust, agreement, and affection for people, and still move the action forward.

The real work here is about creating the space where peace can triumph in the face of our attraction to the clash of cultures and ideologies, intensified by a journalistic megaphone that is primarily interested in what is wrong with the world. It aims for peace in the face of social media outlets where attention is the only goal, celebrity without substance makes the winners, and fabrication without facts is the way to create an audience.

There is much unneeded suffering in the world and in our institutional life, much of it caused by our desire to have our own way or to adapt to what we don't believe in. Collaboration with the enemy is one form of the politics we have been waiting for: a reachable way for power, love, and neighborliness to reshape our collective lives.

Peter Block
December 2016

Preface

I have spent the past twenty-five years helping teams of remarkable people work together on some of the most important challenges of our time: jobs, education, health, food, energy, climate, justice, security, peace. These people have been committed to making progress, and to do so they have been willing to work not only with their colleagues and friends but also with their opponents and enemies: politicians of all parties, guerrillas and army generals, activists and bureaucrats, trade unionists and business executives. When these collaborations succeeded, they produced inspiring breakthroughs, and when they didn't, they produced disappointment and disillusionment. These extraordinary experiences, all around the world, have enabled me to observe, up close and in bright colors, how collaboration works and doesn't work.

Over this same period, I have also, in my daily life, worked together with colleagues, clients, partners, friends, and family. Sometimes I wanted to work with these people and sometimes I didn't. When our collaborations succeeded, I felt happy, and when they didn't, I felt frustrated. Moreover, I felt confused and embarrassed: how could I, an international expert on collaboration, have failed in my own practice? These ordinary experiences have enabled me to observe, also up close but in muted shades, how collaboration works and doesn't work.

The juxtaposition of these two different sets of experiences has surprised me. I have been able to see that the central challenge of collaboration is the same in both extraordinary and ordinary situations. This challenge is simple but not easy: How can we work together with diverse others, including people we don't agree with or like or trust?

This book is for everyone who wrestles with how to get things done with unlike others, whether within their own business or government or nonprofit organization, or with people in other organizations or communities or sectors. It is for everyone who needs to make progress on their most important challenges, not only with their colleagues and friends but also with their opponents and enemies.

Over these past years, I have had many opportunities in many contexts to try to get things done through collaboration. Through much trial and much error, I have gradually been able to understand what it really takes to work together. This book reports what I have learned.

Introduction: How to Work with People You Don't Agree with or Like or Trust

We face the same basic challenge everywhere: at home and work, in business and politics, on community and national and global issues. We are trying to get something done that we think is crucial. To do this, we need to work with others. These others include people we do not agree with or like or trust. And so we are torn: we think that we must work with these others and also that we must not. Collaboration seems both imperative and impossible. What do we do?

The reason such collaborations seem impossible is that we misunderstand collaboration.

Our conventional understanding of collaboration is that it requires us all to be on the same team and headed in the same direction, to agree on what has to happen and make sure this happens, and to get people to do what needs to be done. In other words, we assume that collaboration can and must be under control. Conventional collaboration looks like a planning meeting.

But this conventional assumption is wrong. When we are working in complex situations with diverse others, collaboration cannot and need not be controlled.

Unconventional, *stretch collaboration* abandons the assumption of control. It gives up unrealistic fantasies of harmony,

Two Approaches to Collaboration

	Conventional Collaboration	Stretch Collaboration
How we relate with our collaborators	Focus on the good and harmony of the team (one superior whole)	Embrace conflict and connection (multiple diverse holons)
How we advance our work	Agree on the problem and the solution (one optimum plan)	Experiment our way forward (multiple emergent possibilities)
How we participate in our situation	Change what other people are doing (one paramount leader)	Step into the game (multiple cocreators)

Conventional

Stretch

certainty, and compliance, and embraces messy realities of discord, trial and error, and cocreation. Stretch collaboration looks like martial arts practice. Stretch collaboration enables us to get things done even in complex situations with people we don't agree with or like or trust.

Stretch collaboration requires us to make three fundamental shifts in how we work.

First, in how we relate with our fellow collaborators, we must stretch away from focusing narrowly on the collective goals and harmony of our team, and move toward embracing both conflict and connection within and beyond the team.

Second, in how we advance our work, we must stretch away from insisting on clear agreements about the problem, the solution, and the plan, and move toward experimenting systematically with different perspectives and possibilities.

And third, in how we participate in our situation—in the role we play—we must stretch away from trying to change what other people are doing, and move toward entering fully into the action, willing to change ourselves.

Stretch collaboration is challenging because all three of these stretches require us to do the opposite of what seems natural. Rather than shrink away from complexity we must plunge into it. Often this feels uncomfortable and frightening.

These stretches require us to pluralize: to move away from paying attention only to one dominant whole, one optimum plan, and one superior leader, toward attending to multiple diverse holons (wholes that are part of larger wholes), multiple emergent possibilities, and multiple cocreators.

Getting things done in complex situations with diverse others is never straightforward. Energies must be mobilized; needs must be balanced; actions must be taken. Stretching does not make this work disappear; it just enables us to do it with less fear and distraction and more connection and awareness. The proverb says, "Before enlightenment, chop wood, carry water. After enlightenment, chop wood, carry water." After enlightened stretching, we still have our work to do, but now we have a better chance of doing it successfully.

This book presents a theory and practice of stretch collaboration. Chapter 1 explains why collaboration is necessary and why it is intrinsically difficult. Chapter 2 suggests a way to decide when to collaborate and when instead to force, adapt, or exit. Chapter 3 specifies the limitations of conventional collaboration and the narrow conditions under which it is applicable. Chapter 4 outlines stretch collaboration, and chapters 5, 6, and 7 elaborate the three stretches it entails: embracing conflict and connection, experimenting a way forward, and stepping into the game. The conclusion offers a program of exercises to put these ideas into practice.

1

Collaboration Is Becoming More Necessary and More Difficult

The urge to form partnerships, to link up in collaborative arrangements, is perhaps the oldest, strongest, and most fundamental force in nature. There are no solitary, free living creatures: every form of life is dependent on other forms.

—Lewis Thomas[1]

*C*ollaboration is often imperative and usually challenging. And the more we need it, the more difficult we find it.

"I COULD NEVER WORK WITH *THOSE* PEOPLE!"

In November 2015, I was facilitating the first workshop of a group of 33 national leaders. They had come together to search for solutions to their country's most critical problem: the devastating nexus of insecurity, illegality, and inequality. Everyone at the meeting was worried about this situation and determined to do something about it, and they thought that together they might be able to do more than separately. I thought the project was important and was determined to do a good job.

The participants came from every part of the society: politicians, human rights activists, army generals, business owners, religious leaders, trade unionists, intellectuals, journalists. They had deep ideological differences, and many of them were political or professional or personal rivals. Mostly they didn't agree with or like or trust each other. In the country and in the group, suspicion and defensiveness were sky-high.

To solve their most important problem, these people needed to work together, but they weren't sure they could.

I thought the workshop was going well. The participants were talking about their very different experiences and perspectives, all together and in small groups, and at meals and on walks and on trips outside the hotel to visit local people and projects. They were cautiously starting to get to know one another and to hope that together they could make a difference.

Then, on the final morning, the project organizing team (eleven locals and my colleagues and me) got into an argument about some things that were not going well: methodological confusions, logistical glitches, communication breakdowns. Some of the organizers thought I was doing a bad job, and the next day they wrote a critical note that they circulated among themselves.

One of the team members forwarded the note to me. I felt offended and upset that the organizers were challenging my expertise and professionalism behind my back. I was frightened that the accomplishment and income I was expecting from the project were at risk. I thought I needed to defend myself, so I sent off first one, then a second, and then a third email explaining why, in my expert view, what I had done in the workshop had been correct. I knew that I had made some mistakes but was worried that if I admitted these now, I would be opening myself up to greater danger. I was certain that overall I was right and they were wrong: that they were the villains and I was the victimized hero.

As the week went on and I had phone conversations with different organizers, my attitude hardened. I thought the people who were blaming me for the problems we were having were unconscionably betraying our team effort and me. I fought back and blamed them. I became increasingly suspicious, mistrustful, assertive, and rigid. I also wanted to keep myself safe, so I became increasingly cautious and canny. I decided that I didn't agree with or like or trust these organizers and didn't want to engage with them on this matter or to work with them anymore. What I really wanted was for them to disappear.

THE ENEMYFYING SYNDROME

This short, sharp conflict enabled me to feel in my gut a challenge that I had been thinking about for a long time. In order to make progress on this project, which was important to me, I needed to work with others. These others included people I did not agree with or like or trust. I slipped into thinking of them as my enemies. This polarization within our team put the work we were doing at risk. Moreover, in this small interaction within our team, we reproduced a central dynamic in the larger national system—mistrust, fragmentation, breakdown—that the project had been established to counter.

In this ordinary incident, I enacted a common behavior or syndrome that I call *enemyfying*: thinking and acting as if the people we are dealing with are our enemies—people who are the cause of our problems and are hurting us. In different contexts we use different words with subtly different connotations for the people from whom we differentiate ourselves: *others, rivals, competitors, opponents, adversaries, enemies*. We use these characterizations often, in both ordinary and extraordinary contexts, sometimes thoughtfully and sometimes casually, even habitually. But the enemies are always the others: *those* people. It's like the jokes about the conjugation of irregular verbs, such as "I am firm, you are obstinate, he is a pig-headed fool." The enemyfying equivalent is "I see things differently, you are wrong, she is the enemy."

We see enemyfying all around us. It dominates the media every day: people identifying others not just as opponents to be defeated but as enemies to be destroyed. These others are variously labeled as nationalists and cosmopolitans, immigrants and racists, corporations and environmentalists, terrorists and infidels.

The 2016 US presidential election overflowed with enemyfying. Speaking of Donald Trump's campaign, comedian Aasif Mandvi explained how enemyfying creates a self-perpetuating vicious circle:

> Trump is essentially tapping into the most fearful, racist, xenophobic, fear-based mind-set in this country, but he's also justifying that in other parts of the world. Whether it's ISIS or it's Trump—what they're basically saying is: There's a reason you should be afraid, there's a reason you should feel disenfranchised, there's a reason that you should feel angry, and it's because of those people, over there.[2]

Enemyfying, vilifying, and demonizing pervade political discourse around the world. And we enact this enemyfying syndrome not only in politics but also at work and at home.

I do a lot of enemyfying. I tell myself stories about how other people are messing things up: colleagues, clients, suppliers, neighbors, family. I know that these aren't complete or fair stories about what is happening and that telling these stories isn't a productive way to spend my time. I also know that many people do the same—for example, in couples counseling, which most people enter thinking, "Our problems are my partner's fault, and I hope this counseling makes them understand that they need to change." But enemyfying is seductive because it reassures us that we are OK and not responsible for the difficulties we are facing.

Enemyfying is a way to understand and deal with real differences. It simplifies into black and white our overwhelmingly complex and multihued reality, and thereby enables us to clarify what is going on and mobilize energies to deal with it. But, as journalist H. L. Mencken said, "There is always an easy solution to every human problem—neat, plausible, and wrong."[3] Our enemyfying, which feels exciting and satisfying, even righteous and heroic, usually obscures rather than clarifies the reality of the challenges we face. It amplifies conflicts; it narrows the space for problem solving and creativity; and it distracts us, with unrealizable dreams of decisive victory, from the real work we need to do.

THE CENTRAL CHALLENGE OF COLLABORATION

The enemyfying syndrome that I have observed and enacted is at the heart of the challenge of collaboration.

In politics and at work and at home, collaboration is both necessary and difficult. We want to get something done that is important to us, but to do so, we need to work with people who view things differently than us. And the more important the issue and different the views, the more necessary and difficult the collaboration.

The central challenge of collaboration is crystallized in the tension between its two dictionary definitions. It means simply "to work jointly with," but also "to cooperate traitorously with the enemy."[4] The word therefore evokes both a story of generous and inclusive progress, such as an energetic and creative work team ("We must all collaborate!"), and a story of degenerative and amoral villainy, as in France during World War II ("Death to collaborators!").

The challenge of collaboration is that in order to make our way forward, we *must* work with others, including people we don't agree with or like or trust, while in order to avoid treachery, we must *not* work with them.

This challenge is becoming more acute. People are more free and individualistic and so more diverse, with more voice and less deference. Their identities and affiliations are more fluid. Enabled by new technologies, established political, organizational, social, and familial hierarchies are breaking down. Volatility, uncertainty, complexity, and ambiguity are growing.

Increasingly often, we are therefore unable to get things done unilaterally or only with our colleagues and friends. More and more, we need to work with others, including our opponents and enemies—and we find it more and more difficult to do so.

This collaborative challenge is wonderful in that it grows out of the weakening of authoritarianism and subservience. And it is terrible in that, if we fail to meet it, we will produce ever-increasing fragmentation, polarization, and violence.

We must find a way to collaborate more effectively.

We are face-to-face with the challenge of collaboration when we say, "I could never work with *those* people!" What do we mean by this common exclamation? Maybe we mean that we don't want to work with those people, or that we are not able to, or that we don't need to. In such situations, when we think it is not desirable or possible or necessary to work with certain others, then obviously we will try to work without them or against them: to avoid them or defeat them.

But what do we do when we think it *is* necessary to work with these others? This might be because we worry that we can't avoid or defeat them, or they have some skill or resource that we need, or we believe it would be wrong to exclude them.

Such situations present us with the central challenge of collaboration. We see these other people's values and behaviors as different from ours; we believe they are wrong or bad; we feel frustrated or angry. Although we know that we have to work with them, we wish we didn't. We worry that we will have to compromise or betray what we believe is right and matters most to us. In these situations, although we see that we need to collaborate with those people, we don't see how we can do so successfully.

How can we succeed, then, in working with people we don't agree with or like or trust?

2

Collaboration Is Not the Only Option

The Art of War *is not only about making war. It is in fact a manual for how to work effectively and artfully with extreme and chaotic situations and with any kind of conflict. It not only acknowledges that conflict is inevitable in life but also tells us that we can accomplish our objective without adding to the conflict. That's why people keep coming back to it—not because it tells them how to wage war better but because it tells them that conflict rarely needs to reach the level of "war," where the highly polarized fight exhausts the resources of the parties involved, be they nations, business partners, colleagues, or friends.*

—James Gimian and Barry Boyce[1]

We can't work out *how* to collaborate until we understand *when* to collaborate. Collaboration is only one of four ways that we can approach situations we find problematic. Collaboration is not always our best option.

The way forward is unclear

John and Mary are at their wits' end. Their son Bob has fallen way behind in his mortgage payments again and this time is at risk of losing his home. They are frightened for Bob and his family and also tired of bailing him out. Should they do what they have done before and give him money to make his payments? Should they use the influence they have over him to make him get his act together? Should they cut him off and let him deal with his own mess? Should they work with him to find a way to deal with this situation? They aren't sure what to do.

This simple vignette illustrates the starting point for any attempt to collaborate to deal with a challenging situation. Things are not going as we want them to, and in particular, other people are not doing what we want them to. We have several options. Should we try to collaborate?

"The miraculous option is that we work things through together"

I first became interested in the potential of collaboration as the result of an inspiring experience I had in 1991 in South Africa. At the time, I was working at the London headquarters of the energy company Royal Dutch Shell, where I was responsible for developing global social-political-economic scenarios: alternative stories about what could happen in the company's future business environment. One year earlier, the white government of F. W. de Klerk had released Nelson Mandela from prison and began negotiations to end apartheid and to move to democracy. Two professors at the University of the Western Cape, Pieter le Roux and Vincent Maphai, had the idea of using the Shell scenario methodology to think through how South Africans could effect their national transition. They invited me to provide methodological guidance to this effort. This is how I came to facilitate the Mont Fleur Scenario Exercise.[2]

Le Roux and Maphai decided to do this scenario work not with a team made up only of their colleagues (as we did at Shell) but also with leaders from across the whole segregated society: politicians, businesspeople, trade unionists, community leaders, and academics; black and white; opposition and establishment; from the left and right. I worked with this team over four weekends in 1991 and 1992. I was amazed at how, in spite of their profound differences, they were able to collaborate happily and creatively and to make an important contribution to South Africans achieving a successful transition.

My experience at Mont Fleur upended my understanding of what was possible in the world and in my own life. On my first trip to Cape Town, I heard a joke that exemplified what I was witnessing. "Faced with our country's overwhelming problems," it went, "we have two options: a practical option and a miraculous option. The practical option is for all of us to get down on our knees and pray for a band of angels to come down from heaven and solve our problems for us. The miraculous option is that we work things through together." I loved this joke and repeated it many times over the years that followed. I could see that through collaborating with their enemies, South Africans had succeeding in enacting the miraculous option.

I was so enthusiastic about what I had experienced at Mont Fleur that I quit my job at Shell and emigrated to Cape Town to devote myself to following the thread that I had picked up there. I was certain that collaborating was the best way to address complex challenges. Over the subsequent decades, I led tens of large collaborations all over the world, cofounded a social enterprise to support this work, and wrote three books on the principles and practices that my colleagues and I were discovering.

From time to time over these years, however, I had experiences that raised questions in my mind about the collaborative option. For example, in 2003, agricultural activist Hal Hamilton and I initiated a large-scale collaboration called the Sustainable Food Lab. This effort, which is still going strong, brings together companies such as Unilever, Walmart, and Starbucks, and nongovernmental organizations such as WWF, Oxfam, and the Rainforest Alliance, plus farmers and researchers and government agencies, to accelerate progress toward a more sustainable global food system.[3]

During our first months of convening the initial members of the Sustainable Food Lab, Hamilton and I talked with many food system leaders about whether they would be interested in participating in such an undertaking. Many of them thought it would enable them to make better progress on their own sustainability objectives, and by mid-2004 we had a large and diverse enough team that we could launch the lab.

But one aspect of our convening work struck me: the thoughtful arguments made by three organizations that we invited to join but that declined. One global company said they would prefer to pursue sustainability on their own as a way to obtain a competitive advantage. An international workers' organization said they would be interested in being part of such a group but not until they had built up their power and could engage with the participating corporations as equals. And a government agency said they saw their role as working apart from other organizations so that they could make and enforce regulations without being accused of bias. All three of these actors had reasons why collaboration was not their best option.

Meanwhile, on and off from 2000 to 2012, I tried to help some Venezuelan colleagues organize a broad multistakeholder collaboration to address the severe economic, social, and political challenges facing their country. But time after time, our efforts ran up against the unwillingness of Hugo Chávez's revolutionary socialist government to participate in our project, so it never got off the ground.

In 2011, a congressman from a Venezuelan opposition party told me a story about the extraordinary level of political noncollaboration. "The government and the opposition members of Congress used to be able to work together in certain committees," he said, "but now the government refuses to talk with us at all. The only conversation I have had recently with a Chavista was in the privacy of a men's room in the Congress, where one of them standing at the adjacent urinal whispered to me, 'If you guys get into power, don't forget that we're friends, right?'"

What I eventually understood was that the refusal of the Chávez government to participate in our project was not because they didn't understand the principles or opportunities of collaboration. We didn't need to explain it again, more carefully and convincingly. They refused because their strategy was based in part on an opposite logical premise: that demonizing their political opponents as treasonous capitalist elites helped them retain the support of their popular base. In this case, then, from the perspective of the Chavistas (like other politicians in other countries), collaboration was not their best option.

And over this period, while I was trying to help other people with their collaborations, I was having problems in my own. I had lots of difficulties getting along with people, and long, quiet, sad estrangements. Three times I had a drawn-out conflict with a different one of my business partners. In each case, we had disagreements that become more harsh and sour, and which we were not able to resolve. These experiences left me puzzled and embarrassed: I was worried that my inability to work out my ordinary conflicts meant that I was a fraud in guiding others to work out their extraordinary ones.

THERE ARE THREE ALTERNATIVES TO COLLABORATION

It was only many years later, in Thailand, that I understood clearly what is involved in choosing to collaborate.

In August 2010, I went to Bangkok at the invitation of a group of citizens who were worried about the ongoing political conflict between pro- and antigovernment forces, which had recently produced bloody protests. They were frightened that the unrest, polarization, and violence might spiral out of control—in the worst case into civil war. This group convened a team of leaders from across Thai politics, business, the military, the aristocracy, and civil society organizations, who represented many factions in the conflict and who mostly blamed each other for what was going wrong. They were, however, willing to work together on a question that mattered to all of them: "What kind of Thailand do we want to leave for our children?"

I participated in these workshops and also in many smaller meetings with different actors, trying to help them find ways to resolve the conflict. In its particulars, Thailand's history and culture and values are unique and, for me, were bewildering. But Thais are also wrestling with social dynamics that are present around the world, so working with this team enabled me to learn general lessons about what it takes to deal with these dynamics.

The team worked between April and August 2013 to make sense of what was going on in their country. They shared their varied experiences and understandings with one another and also met with academic experts and ordinary people. Out of this immersion they discerned three complex challenges that Thailand faces: social and cultural tensions, economic and environmental pressures, and political and institutional constraints. They agreed that the future that would unfold in Thailand would depend not so much on the specifics of *what* Thais did to address these challenges as on *how* they addressed them.

The team said there were three basic stances toward their country's challenges that Thais could take. They named these stances We Adapt, We Force, and We Collaborate.

In We Adapt, Thais would simply get on with looking after themselves and their families and organizations, and leave addressing the larger societal challenges to others, especially the government and elites. This was the approach that most individuals and organizations were used to taking.

In We Force, many people would become involved in political movements to push for or impose top-down solutions to these challenges. They would fight to win. Thais had taken this stance in the past, most recently during the political unrest of 2008–2010.

And in We Collaborate, many people would get involved in new cross-factional and cross-sectoral efforts to develop a multitude of bottom-up solutions. This approach had the least precedent in Thailand.

The team's primary conclusion was that Thais would be unable to address their complex challenges if the dominant stance they took was either of the two most familiar ones, We Adapt or We Force. The challenges were too complex and the society too polarized for a successful way forward to be dictated from the top down by any particular faction of experts and authorities. They would be able to address their challenges only if the stance they took was the less familiar and more inclusive We Collaborate. The team then created a movement in Thailand to build this capacity, which they called Collaborate We Can. I was happy with these conclusions because they accorded with my long-held belief in collaboration.

In November 2013, I returned to Thailand to help the team finish writing up our report. Our thinking about what could happen in the country was, however, quickly being overtaken by what we could see on television was actually happening. The government had attempted to pass a law to give amnesty to politicians for offenses committed during previous periods of unrest, and hundreds of thousands of antigovernment protesters who thought this law was corrupt organized mass rallies, pushed their way into government buildings, and demanded that the elected parliament be replaced by an appointed council. Mutual enemy-fying escalated, with each side denouncing its opponents as irrational, bad, or traitorous. The worst fear of the Thai team, that the country would descend into civil war, now seemed possible.

I was alarmed and disappointed at this collapse of efforts to enact a We Collaborate scenario. Even more, I was surprised that so many of my Thai colleagues, convinced that at this juncture collaboration meant capitulation, were working to enact different variations of We Force through their enthusiastic support for either pro- or antigovernment actions.

Throughout the first months of 2014, the political conflict in Thailand continued in the parliament, the courts, and the streets. The antigovernment protestors occupied parts of central Bangkok, seized government buildings, and forcibly prevented the election of a new government. The government declared a state of emergency and tried to close down occupied sites. The two sides held talks to try to resolve the conflict, but these failed. Finally, in May 2014, the army implemented their own We Force option: they staged a coup, established a junta to govern the country, declared martial law, censored the media, and arrested politicians and activists—including some from our team.

Over these months of Thai history, then, the three options the team had described had all been in play. But as the national crisis intensified, many Thais abandoned We Adapt and We Collaborate for We Force. They saw collaboration with their opponents and enemies as unpalatable. They did not see collaboration as their best option.

Over the months that followed, I spoke many times with my Thai colleagues about what had happened and what it meant. The more we talked about the thinking of the team, the more valuable I found it. I came to believe that the team had uncovered an archetypal framework for the options that are available, not only to Thais but to all of us, to deal with the challenging situations we face.

Collaboration Must Be a Choice

What I came to understand in Thailand was that whenever we are faced with a situation we find problematic, in politics or at work or at home, we have four ways that we can respond: collaborating, forcing, adapting, or exiting. (The Thai team did not discuss exiting because they were focused on how to effect

Four Ways to Deal with Problematic Situations

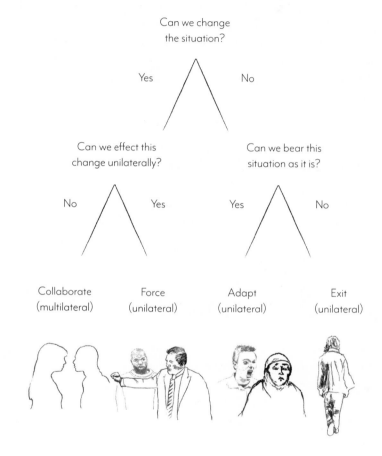

Can we change
the situation?

Yes   No

Can we effect this   Can we bear this
change unilaterally?   situation as it is?

No   Yes   Yes   No

Collaborate   Force   Adapt   Exit
(multilateral)   (unilateral)   (unilateral)   (unilateral)

change from within the country.) Sometimes not all of these options are available to us; for example, we may not have the means to employ forcing. But we always have to choose from among these four options.

Many people think of collaboration as the best and right default option: that we are all interconnected and interdependent and ought to work together. This was the lesson I took from Mont Fleur, but I now think it is only sometimes true. We can't always work with everyone or never work with anyone, so collaboration is not always right or always wrong. In practice, we have to decide in each situation whether or not to collaborate.

We may make this decision rationally or intuitively or habitually, but in any event we must have a clear understanding of the opportunities and risks of each option.

We try *collaborating* when we want to change the situation we are in and think that we can do so only if we work with others (multilaterally). We think that we cannot alone know what needs to be done or that, even if we can know, we cannot alone succeed in getting it done. We may or may not want to collaborate—but we think that, under the circumstances, we need to.

Collaborating presents the opportunity, as we work with others—perhaps opponents and enemies as well as colleagues and friends—to find a more effective way forward and have a larger and more sustained impact on our situation. But collaborating is not a panacea: the risk it presents is that it will produce too little too slowly—that it will lead to our compromising too much, or even being coopted and betraying what matters to us most. In the early 1990s, for example, South Africans chose to collaborate, at Mont Fleur and elsewhere, to effect a negotiated transition to democracy. Most of them believed this was the best option—but this decision and the compromises it entailed were contested then and are even more so now.

We try *forcing* when we think that we ought to and may be able to change our situation without working with others (unilaterally). We think that we, alone or together with our colleagues and friends, know best what needs to be done, and must and can impose this on others. We can do this imposing in many different ways: peacefully or violently; by enticing or defeating; using our ideas, skills, supporters, votes, authority, money, or weapons.

The opportunity of forcing is that it accords with a way of thinking that for many people is natural and habitual. They believe that in most situations, forcing is the best—perhaps even the only realistic—way to effect change; that in principle it is right to use force for a just cause, and that not to do so would be wrong and cowardly. The risk of forcing is that as we try to push through what we think needs to be done, others who think differently will push back, and therefore we will not achieve the outcome we intend. In 2014, the two sides in the Thai conflict tried to force the outcome they wanted, and then the military forced theirs. Many people agreed with the military's action because it prevented the violence from escalating, but it produced only halting progress in addressing the country's challenges.

We try *adapting* when we think that we cannot change our situation and so we need to find a way to live with it. Adapting may require us to employ lots of intelligence and ingenuity and courage, but we do this within a limited sphere. We believe that we are not able to change what is happening outside our immediate area of influence; we cannot change the rules of the game, so we must play it as well as we can. We therefore focus on doing the best we can and ignore or avoid or fit into what is happening around us.

The opportunity of adapting is that we can get on with living our life without expending energy on trying to change things we cannot. Sometimes adapting works just fine for us, and sometimes it does not work fine but it is the best we can do. The risk is that the situation we are in is so inhospitable that we will be unable to adapt and will struggle even to survive. The three parties that declined to participate in the Sustainable Food Lab thought they could achieve their objectives best if they worked within the system as it was, rather than entering into a novel collaboration to try to transform it.

We try *exiting* when we think we cannot change our situation and we are no longer willing to live with it. We can exit through quitting, divorcing, or walking away. Sometimes exiting is simple and easy, and sometimes it requires us to give up a lot that matters to us. In Venezuela, more than one million people despaired of the crisis in their country and emigrated.

This elaboration of the four options enabled me to understand better what I had been doing during the times I had conflicts with my business partners. First, I would try adapting: seeking a way to do what I wanted to do while fitting into the status quo of the partnership—going along to get along. When this didn't work, I would try collaborating to change the status quo, but I wasn't able to make this work. I was afraid of conflict—worried that I would get hurt or lose face—so I shrank from it, attempting to keep things polite and under control. This prevented me from resolving our disagreements in a way that allowed us to continue to work together, and because I found the conflict so uncomfortable, I didn't see how we could continue to work together if we couldn't agree. In the end, I would try forcing: trying to get things to be the way I wanted them to be, even if my partner didn't. In some of these cases, I won and my opponent was forced out of the partnership, and sometimes I was the one who exited.

We can view our choice among these four options through the pragmatic lens of power. From this perspective, we choose to collaborate only when it is the best way to achieve our objectives. More specifically, we choose the multilateral option of collaborating when the unilateral options of adapting and exiting are unpalatable and the unilateral option of forcing is impossible. Put another way, we adapt or exit when others are more powerful than us and so can force things to be the way they want them to be; we force when we are the more powerful; and we collaborate only when our power is evenly matched and neither of us can impose our will.

Of course, we cannot choose to collaborate all by ourselves. It is easy to begin to collaborate when we and the others all agree that we need to and want to. But often we want to collaborate and the others don't (or vice versa). The others are making the assessment that exiting or adapting (not dealing with us) or forcing (defeating us) is a better option than collaborating (working with us). In such circumstances, we can wait for their frustration, doubt, or desperation about the viability of their unilateral options, and hence their interest in collaborating, to increase. Or we can act to increase their frustration, doubt, or desperation about the viability of their unilateral options—for example, by demonstrating that we are willing and able to employ countervailing force. Or we can act to increase their excitement, curiosity, or hope about the viability of collaborating—for example, by getting a third party to guarantee the safety of the activity.

Finally, we may decide to collaborate not only because of the characteristics of the specific situation we are in, but also because of our general preferences. We may have reasons—political, social, cultural, psychological, spiritual—to prefer to be in collaboration and community and communion.

Collaborating is not our only option, so we need to think clearheadedly about whether, in any given situation, to choose it or forcing or adapting or exiting. But let's say that, through whatever combination of reason and intuition and preference, we choose to collaborate. We then face the next question: How can we do this successfully?

3

Conventional, Constricted
Collaboration Is Becoming Obsolete

The difficulty lies, not in the new ideas, but in escaping from the old ones, which ramify, for those brought up as most of us have been, into every corner of our minds.

—John Maynard Keynes[1]

*O*ur most common default mode for collaborating is controlled. But in most complex and contentious contexts, this mode does not and cannot work.

CONSTRICTION PREVENTS MOVEMENT

John and Mary are talking about what to do about their son Bob's financial problems. They want to help, and they also know from experience that they can't force him to do anything. They don't want to fight either with each other or with Bob. So they need to find a way to work this out together.

John takes a directive approach. He thinks that Bob has been messing up his life for a long time and that they need to get him to sort things out once and for all. Mary thinks that Bob is having a tough time with his business and that they ought to give him some money so that his children don't suffer, but she is willing to go along with John. They agree on a narrow compromise: they will give Bob the money he needs to catch up on his mortgage but also make it clear to him that this will be the last time.

John arranges to meet Bob for lunch, listens to Bob's explanation of his situation, and then in a sympathetic voice tells Bob what he and Mary have decided they are willing to do to help out. Bob feels defensive but thanks John, accepts the offer, and promises to be more careful with his money.

Bob returns home to his wife, Jane. He tells her that he is relieved to have gotten some help but that he resents the way his parents treat him like a child. He doesn't know how to change what he is doing, so his financial problems recur. John and Mary feel taken advantage of and disappointed. All four of them retreat; they spend less time together and their relationships become cooler. They have not made any progress on their issues—in fact, they now feel even more frustrated and angry.

Change management assumes control

In all of my first jobs and many of my first consulting projects, I worked for large organizations: corporations, government agencies, research institutes. So I understand how such organizations typically do things. Here is a composite story of an organizational change process.

Susan Jones is the CEO of a large hospital that is facing disorienting changes in its social and economic and technological environment, and is producing consistently poor clinical and financial results. She gets her board to approve a comprehensive project to transform the hospital's operations. She knows that this transformation will require many professionals—doctors, nurses, researchers, technicians, administrators—to make many changes in what they are doing, and that she will therefore not be able to direct or impose this effort unilaterally. So she decides to undertake this project collaboratively.

Jones sets up a transformation team that includes the hospital's top twenty-five managers from across all departments. She organizes an off-site workshop so that they can jell as a team and agree on a plan for the transformation. She hires expert consultants to diagnose the hospital's problem, prescribe a solution, and present their report to the workshop. She focuses the workshop discussions on what will be best for the patients and for the hospital as a whole, insisting that her managers put aside their parochial departmental agendas.

At the end of this workshop, the team has reached consensus on a plan to implement the solution recommended by the consultants. It specifies what each department must do in order to effect the transformation and also the incentives and sanctions that will ensure its implementation on time and on budget. Jones and her team are pleased with having accomplished this important and complicated task.

Jones sends out an email to all hospital staff announcing the rollout of the transformation. But most of them greet this communication with cynicism and defensiveness. They doubt that it will work, they worry that they will have to compromise their professional standards, and they fear that their jobs will become less satisfying and secure. They blame Jones, their managers, the consultants, and people in other departments. Public health officials and patients also raise concerns in the newspapers and on social media.

As the managers begin to implement their plan, they run into unexpected complications, delays, resistance, and overruns. The managers push the implementation harder, but the effort becomes more stuck. Clinical and financial results deteriorate further. Finally, the board declares that the transformation project has failed and they cancel it. Recriminations abound.

In implementing this collaborative transformation, Jones made three typical mistakes.

First, she focused all of the conversations about this project on the good and interests of the hospital as a whole. In doing this, she papered over the crucial fact that different departments and individuals had radically different perspectives on what was happening and ought to happen, and that the transformation would produce winners and losers. Jones also overlooked the inconvenient fact that, in conversations about "the good of the whole," it was true only for her that the interests of the whole and her own interests (her compensation and career) were identical—everyone else's interests depended largely on what happened to their department and their job. It was not true that there was only one whole to be optimized: there were many wholes to be managed, and to suggest otherwise was simplistic and manipulative.

Jones's second mistake was that, in trying to advance the transformation, she and her consultants pushed to articulate a single statement of the problem, the solution, and the plan. But the hospital's situation was too complex, with too many people having their own perspectives and proposals, for them to be able to obtain an agreement that was substantive and sincere. And not only could they not get agreement on what would work, they could not know what would work before they tried it out: lots of people had opinions but no one actually knew. The real work of the transformation was not to choose among existing fixed options but to cocreate new options as the work unfolded.

The third mistake was in how Jones and her managers and consultants saw what they needed to do to effect this transformation. They thought that change management meant getting other people—subordinates, suppliers, patients—to change their values and thinking and actions. This fundamentally hierarchical assumption, that higher people change lower people, makes everyone defensive: people don't dislike change, but they dislike being changed. This transformation would require everyone to be open to learning and changing.

"There is only one right answer"

All of my training was to be an expert problem solver. In 1979, I started an undergraduate degree in physics at McGill University in my hometown of Montreal, proud to be in such a brainy field. I enjoyed spending my evenings calculating solutions to mathematical problems. I got perfect marks on exams because beforehand I had worked through the correct answer to every question in the textbooks.

In the summer of 1981 I attended a global conference of scientists concerned with big problems such as nuclear war. I wrote a conference paper that made a logical but naïve argument for using planes rather than satellites to monitor compliance with arms treaties. One of my mentors used a phrase to criticize my paper that I had never heard before: "Don't let the best be the enemy of the good." I was surprised by this notion that there was not simply one correct answer.

At this conference, I heard a presentation on the environmental problems of energy production and was attracted to working on such an important public issue. So in 1982, I started a graduate degree in energy and environmental economics at the University of California, Berkeley, that trained students in the rational assessment of complex policy issues. My master's thesis proved that the Brazilian government program to substitute sugar-based alcohol for gasoline was uneconomical. Then I got a series of research postings in the United States, France, Austria, and Japan. In each of these places, I was given the same kind of assignment: figure out, for some complex issue, the optimum policy response.

After I graduated from Berkeley in 1986, I was hired as a corporate planning coordinator at Pacific Gas & Electric Company in San Francisco. The essence of my job was to come up with quick and succinct answers to business questions posed by the company's executives. Once I attended a strategic planning retreat of the company's executive committee and was shocked to see them make decisions based not only on the analyses that my colleagues and I had prepared, but also on habit, politics, and game playing.

Then in 1988, at twenty-seven years old, I got a job in the global planning department of Royal Dutch Shell. During these years, the most common feedback I got was that I was intelligent but arrogant, which I thought was an acceptable trade-off. Shell people had a similar reputation, so when I got there, I thought I fit right in.

Shell's planning department was staffed with bright people recruited from across the company and from external think tanks. Our job was to challenge Shell executives to pay attention to changes in the world that could present new business risks and opportunities. We did this by constructing scenarios of possible futures through reading and talking with people from around the world and then arguing among ourselves, for months and months, about what we were observing and what it meant. The window of my office looked down on the British Houses of Parliament, and I fancied that we, like the parliamentarians, were employing robust and reasoned debate to find the best answers.

By the time I was at Shell, then, I was confident that I knew how to solve complex problems. The model I had internalized from all of my training had three basic steps. First, smart people think through the problem and the solution and make a plan to execute this solution. Second, they get the people in authority to approve this plan. Third, the authorities instruct their subordinates to execute the plan. This all seemed obvious and reasonable to me. Later, my boss at Shell, Kees van der Heijden, explained that this model provides the foundation for all conventional strategic planning; it falls into

> the rationalist school, which codifies thought and action
> separately. The tacit underlying assumption is that there

is one best solution, and the job of the strategist is to get as close to this as possible within the limited resources available. Having decided the optimal way forward, the question of strategy implementation is addressed separately.[2]

THE LIMITATIONS OF CONVENTIONAL COLLABORATION

After my experience at Mont Fleur, I left Shell to work on collaborative efforts to address complex public challenges. Almost everyone I worked with—in governments, companies, and nonprofits, around the world—was implicitly using some variation of the three-step conventional, rationalistic, linear, hierarchical model that I had learned.

I tried to make this model work in my collaborations, but it didn't.

What I observed was that people who come together to work on a complex challenge almost never follow these three steps, even if they think they are supposed to. They often produce useful outputs—new relationships, insights, commitments, initiatives, and capacities—but they rarely do this through executing an agreed-upon plan. Sometimes they produce some outputs and sometimes others; sometimes they end up doing something close to what they originally intended and sometimes they make radical changes; sometimes they are able to work together only briefly and sometimes they end up continuing for years; sometimes they move forward in alignment and sometimes in fierce contestation. In practice, they figure out what to do as they go along.

For a long time, I thought the unpredictability of these collaborations could be remedied by participants' being more explicit or disciplined about following the three steps: by doubling down on planning and control. But eventually I realized that the model I had always thought was normal simply does not and cannot work in complex and conflictual situations.

Later I learned that, in transposing the way I had worked on physics problems to my work on policy and strategy, I was making a common mistake. In 1973, Horst Rittel and Melvin Webber wrote:

> The search for scientific bases for confronting problems of social policy is bound to fail, because of the nature of these problems. They are "wicked" problems, whereas science has developed to deal with "tame" problems. Policy problems cannot be definitively described. Moreover, in a pluralistic society there is nothing like the undisputable public good; there is no objective definition of equity; policies that respond to social problems cannot be meaningfully correct or false; and it makes no sense to talk about "optimal solutions" to social problems. Even worse, there are no "solutions" in the sense of definitive and objective answers.[3]

Once I started to question the conventional problem-solving model I had been using, I realized how unsuitable it was for the collaborations I was trying to support.

The difficulty starts with the assumption that there is one right answer. Being certain that we know the right answer doesn't leave much room for other people's answers and therefore makes it more difficult to work together. I saw a vivid example of this in 2010 when I made my first visit to Thailand. My hosts had organized back-to-back meetings over three days with thirty top leaders from across Thai society. A few months earlier, pro- and antigovernment forces had clashed violently in Bangkok, and in these meetings we heard radically different accounts of what had happened and why and who was to blame. I found this series of disjointed conversations to be confusing. But on reflection, I realized that one thread ran through each of the accounts we had heard. In one way or another, every single person had said, "The truth of this situation is . . ."

This is the typical starting point for attempts to collaborate in complex and contentious situations. Usually most of the people involved are convinced that they know the truth about their situation. They are right and others are wrong; they are innocent and others are guilty; and if only the others would listen to and agree with them, then the situation would be rectified. In hierarchical systems such as Pacific Gas & Electric and Thailand, this level of certainty can be dangerous. A belief that "I am right and you are wrong" can easily slip into "I deserve to be superior and you to be inferior." This is a recipe not for generative collaboration but for degenerative imposition.

We hold on to being right to protect our sense of who we are. In 2009, while I was attending the international climate change negotiations in Copenhagen, I had a brief conversation with Berlin researcher Anja Koehne. She was criticizing the German stance toward other countries in the negotiations and used a phrase that penetrated me like an arrow: "feeling superior as a condition of being." This phrase showed me that I was attached to winning arguments and being right, in part because I saw being superior as integral to my identity. I feared that if I was wrong, I would lose a vital part of who I was: that I would not just fail but *be* a failure. I could not relax my grip on having the right answer until I could relax my identification with success.

The typical starting point for collaborating in complex and contentious situations, then, is that the participants do not agree on what the solution is or even on what the problem is. They each have their own truth about what is going on and why, and who needs to do what about it. One way to approach this situation is to understand the participants as the blind men with the elephant. In this fable, the blind man who feels a leg says the elephant is like a pillar, the one who feels the tail says the elephant is like a rope, the one who feels the side says the elephant is like a wall, and so on. This metaphor suggests that each of the participants in a collaboration has a different perspective on the situation that they are all part of and care about, and that if each reveals his or her perspective, then together they can construct a more complete picture.

But the construction of a single agreed-upon model of the whole situation is often not possible. Futurist Don Michael points out that

> in today's world the most advanced among us know about little more than one small piece of the elephant, and there are now so many different pieces, they change so rapidly and they are all so intimately related one to another, that even if we had the technology to put them all together, we would still not be able to make sense of the whole.[4]

So we need to do something more than simply fit together different truths to form a single larger truth.

Political philosopher Isaiah Berlin takes this argument further. He says that trying to agree on and implement a single set of understandings and values is not only unachievable but dangerous:

> If you are truly convinced that there is some solution to all human problems, that one can conceive an ideal society which men can reach if only they do what is necessary to attain it, then you and your followers must believe that no price can be too high to pay in order to open the gates of such a paradise.
>
> The root conviction which underlies this is that the central questions of human life, individual or social, have one true answer which can be discovered. This idea is false. Not only because the solutions given by different schools of social thought differ, and none can be demonstrated by rational methods—but for an even deeper reason. The central values by which most men have lived, in a great many lands at a great many

times—these values, almost if not entirely universal, are not always harmonious with each other.

So we must weigh and measure, bargain, compromise, and prevent the crushing of one form of life by its rivals. I know only too well that this is not a flag under which idealistic and enthusiastic young men and women may wish to march—it seems too tame, too reasonable, too bourgeois and it does not engage the generous emotions. The denial of this, the search for a single, overarching ideal because it is the one and only true one for humanity, invariably leads to coercion. And then to destruction, blood.[5]

Collaborating with diverse others therefore cannot and must not require agreeing on a single truth or answer or solution. Instead, it involves finding a way to move forward together in the absence of or beyond such agreements. This is true not only at work but also at home. The research done by marriage therapist John Gottman, and discussed by Michael Fulwiler, suggests,

69% of relationship conflict is about perpetual problems. All couples have them—these problems are grounded in the fundamental differences that any two people face. They are either 1) fundamental differences in your personalities that repeatedly create conflict, or 2) fundamental differences in your lifestyle needs. In our research, we concluded that instead of solving their perpetual problems, what seems to be important is whether or not a couple can establish a dialogue about them. If they cannot establish such a dialogue, the conflict becomes gridlocked, and gridlocked conflict eventually leads to emotional disengagement.[6]

So the conventional approach to collaboration that I learned in the first part of my career is of limited use. It works only in simple, controlled situations where everyone agrees or goes along and where their actions produce the results they intend. In most social systems—families, organizations, communities, nations—complexity is increasing and control is decreasing, so such situations occur less frequently.

Conventional collaboration is therefore becoming obsolete.

We get into trouble when we incorrectly assume that the situation we are dealing with is simple and controllable, and therefore that conventional collaboration is applicable. In these circumstances, we employ conventional collaboration because it is familiar and comfortable, and we *know* it works. But it does not work: it increases enemyfying and makes our situation even less workable. This causes us to instinctively tense up and double down on conventional collaboration. "It ain't what you don't know that gets you into trouble," the quip goes, "it's what you know for sure that just ain't so."

Conventional collaboration works only in simple, controlled situations. In other situations we need to stretch.

out of control

4

Unconventional, Stretch Collaboration
Is Becoming Essential

*One doesn't discover new lands without consenting to lose sight of
the shore for a very long time.*

—André Gide[1]

For most people, stretch collaboration is unfamiliar
and uncomfortable.

STRETCHING CREATES FLEXIBILITY
AND DISCOMFORT

John and Mary are dealing with their son Bob, who has again
fallen behind on his mortgage payments. But this time they are
trying to employ stretch instead of conventional collaboration.

The three of them feel a loving family connection, but they
also admit that they are coming at this situation with different experiences and perspectives and needs. They talk openly
and vehemently about these differences: John says that he feels
angry and helpless in the face of his son's problems; Mary says
that she is worried for her grandchildren and also that her and
John's own plans for a comfortable retirement will be put in

jeopardy; and Bob says that he is putting all of his energy into his struggling small business and wishes that his family would be supportive rather than only critical. This fight is upsetting and also relieving: they still don't see eye to eye, but they all feel better understood.

They realize that they do not agree on what their real problem is or on what the solution is—maybe they never will agree and maybe they actually don't know. But they are willing to try out some modest new actions that they think could help. John guarantees a bank loan to Bob's company; Mary helps Bob's wife, Jane, look for a job; the two couples talk together about their situation; Bob and John spend Saturdays together with the grandchildren. It's not that their challenges suddenly get easier, but their greater openness enables them to see and try out some new possibilities. Bob and Jane's finances start to improve.

The four of them also back off from trying to change what the others are doing—which, in any case, has not been successful. Instead, they each consider what they themselves might do differently. John makes an effort to connect with Bob on matters other than finances; Mary stands up to John more strongly; Bob talks with a small-business advisor; and Jane takes control of their household budget.

These shifts all help lessen the anger and frustration they feel toward one another and toward their situation. The financial and emotional pressures on them have not gone away and could still overwhelm them. But now they are more able to deal with these pressures thoughtfully and as a family.

All of them find this shift from conventional to stretch collaboration to be difficult. They feel uncomfortable to be stretching: opening up both to greater conflict and to more genuine connection, trying out unfamiliar new actions that may not work, and accepting their own roles in and responsibilities for what is happening. But they are hopeful that this different approach will work better.

How to End a Civil War

If we cannot address our challenges through forcing, adapting, or exiting, then we will need to employ collaboration. And if our challenge is complex and contentious, then the conventional approach to collaboration will not work and we will need to employ an unconventional one.

My experience in South Africa in 1991 gave me a glimpse of such an unconventional approach. But it was only later, in Colombia, that I was able to make out clearly how this new approach worked and how it differed from the conventional one I had been trained in.

Colombia was, since the 1960s, one of the most violent countries in the world, with armed clashes among the military, the police, two left-wing guerrilla armies, right-wing paramilitary vigilantes, drug traffickers, and criminal gangs. This conflict killed hundreds of thousands of civilians and forced millions to flee their homes.

In 1996, a young politician named Juan Manuel Santos visited South Africa and met with Nelson Mandela, who told him about the Mont Fleur project. Santos thought that such a collaboration might help Colombians find a way out of their conflict. He organized a meeting in Bogotá to discuss this possibility and invited me to participate.

The meeting involved generals, politicians, professors, and company presidents. Several leaders of the Revolutionary Armed Forces of Colombia (FARC) participated by radio from a hiding place in the mountains. The participants were both excited and nervous to find themselves in such a heterogeneous group. One Communist Party city councilor, spotting a paramilitary warlord across the room, asked Santos, "Do you really expect me to sit down with this man, who has tried to have me killed five times?" Santos replied, "It is precisely so that he does not do so a sixth time that I am inviting you to sit down."[2]

Out of this meeting the collaborative project named Destino Colombia was initiated.[3] An organizing committee convened a

team of forty-two people that represented the conflict in minia-
ture: military officers, guerrillas, and paramilitaries; activists and
politicians; businesspeople and trade unionists; landowners and
peasants; academics, journalists, and young people.

This team met three times over four months, for a total of
ten days, at a rustic inn outside of Medellín. Both of the illegal, armed, left-wing guerrilla groups, the FARC and the smaller
National Liberation Army (ELN), participated. Although the
government offered them safe passage to the workshops, the
guerrillas thought this would be too risky, so we arranged for
them to participate in the team's meetings by telephone. Three
men called in from the political prisoners' wing of a maximum-
security prison and one from exile in Costa Rica.

Most members of the team were talking with the guerrillas
for the first time and were frightened of retribution for what
they might say. We communicated using two speakerphones in
the meeting room. When people walked by the speakerphones,
they gave the phones a wide berth, afraid to get too close. When
I mentioned this fear, one of the guerrillas observed that our
microcosm was reflecting the macrocosm: "Mr. Kahane, why
are you surprised that people in the room are frightened? The
whole country is frightened." Then he promised that the guerrillas would not kill anyone for anything said in the meetings.

Jaime Caicedo was the secretary general of the far-left
Colombian Communist Party, and Iván Duque was a commander of the far-right paramilitary United Self-Defense Forces
of Colombia (AUC). One evening, Caicedo and Duque stayed
up late talking and drinking and playing the guitar with Juan
Salcedo, a retired army general. The next morning, Caicedo
wasn't in the meeting room when we were due to start, and I
asked the group where he was. They made jokes about what
might have happened to him. One person said, "The general
made him sing." Then Duque said, menacingly, "I saw him
last." I was concerned that Caicedo had been murdered and was
relieved when a few minutes later he walked into the room.

(Years later I heard a revealing coda to this story. Duque had gone into the jungle to meet his boss, Carlos Castaño, the notorious head of AUC. Castaño excitedly told Duque that AUC fighters had discovered the location of their archenemy Caicedo and were on their way to assassinate him. Duque pleaded for Caicedo's life, telling Castaño the story of that evening together at the scenario workshop and saying, "You can't kill him; we were on the Destino Colombia team together." After much arguing, Castaño called off the assassination. I interpreted this story as exemplifying the transformative potential of such collaborations: to be willing to defy Castaño on this matter of life and death, Duque must have transformed his sense of his relationship with Caicedo and of what he himself needed to stand for and do.)

As the work progressed, the team members became less afraid and more willing to speak frankly. Businessman César De Hart said that he had firsthand experience of the conflict with the guerrillas, did not trust them at all, and believed that the country's best hope for peace would be to intensify the military campaign against them. It took courage for him to say this because he was directly challenging not only the guerrillas but also the rest of the team and their hopeful belief that a peaceful solution was possible. He was willing to be open and confrontational, and the team's relationships were now strong enough to hear such a statement without rupturing. Furthermore, when De Hart said exactly what he was thinking and feeling, the fog of conceptual and emotional confusion that had filled the room lifted, and we could all see clearly this mistrust and the possibility of intensified conflict that it implied.

By the end of their third workshop, the team had agreed on four scenarios. The first, "When the Sun Rises We'll See," was a warning of the chaos that would result if Colombians just let things be and failed to address their tough challenges (this scenario, in terms of the Thai framework, exemplified adapting). The second, "A Bird in the Hand Is Worth Two in the Bush," was a story of a negotiated compromise between the government and the guerrillas (conventional collaborating). The third, "Forward March!" was the story foreshadowed in De Hart's suggestion that the government crush the guerrillas militarily and pacify the country (forcing). The fourth, "In Unity Lies Strength," was a story of a bottom-up transformation of the country's mentality toward greater mutual respect and cooperation (stretch collaborating). The team did not agree on which solution to the conflict was most likely or best, so they presented these narratives to their fellow citizens, in newspaper articles and television broadcasts and small and large meetings all around the country, simply as alternative possibilities.

After Destino Colombia, my Colombian colleagues organized several follow-up multistakeholder processes that I facilitated. In one meeting, a group was wrestling with a difficult issue when a politician demanded that they agree on a certain point of principle. I thought that such an agreement would not be possible at that time and urged the group to carry on without agreement, and they did. I was surprised that by the end of the meeting they had agreed to work together on several initiatives, notwithstanding their earlier nonagreement.

The next day, I related this puzzling incident to Antanas Mockus, a former mayor of Bogotá. "Often we do not need to have a consensus on or even to discuss principles," he said. "The most robust agreements are those that different actors support for different reasons." I now understood that people who have deep disagreements can still get important things done together. The bar for making progress on complex challenges is therefore not as high as most people think: we do not need to agree on what the solution is or even on what the problem is.

Over the decades that followed, I was gratified to see that the scenarios and the extraordinary process that produced them remained a touchstone in conversations among Colombians about what they could and should do. At different times over these years, each of the four scenarios seemed to explain what was happening in the country, so these narratives continued to help Colombians make sense of their situation. In 2010, Santos was elected president of the country, and he characterized his government's program as an enactment of "In Unity Lies Strength."

In 2016, Santos finally succeeded in negotiating a peace treaty with the FARC and initiating one with the ELN, and for this he was awarded the Nobel Peace Prize. On the day of this award, his official website posted a note that characterized the first meeting he had organized with me twenty years before as "one of the most significant events in the country's search for peace."[4]

I knew that over the intervening years there had been many different large-scale efforts to resolve the conflict, so I was surprised at the significance that Santos assigned to Destino Colombia. I asked Alberto Fergusson, a psychiatrist and friend of Santos, about this. Fergusson's explanation was that for Santos, the crucial lesson of Destino Colombia, which had animated his political work ever since, was that—contrary to received wisdom —it *is* possible for people who hold contradictory positions to find ways to work together.

The Destino Colombia project helped Colombians work together in a way that contributed to ending a fifty-two-year civil war. This project exemplifies in three ways the stretch approach to collaboration.

First, the Destino Colombia team members were not simply trying to solve one single problem or to optimize one superordinate good, even though their rhetoric was that they were collaborating for the good of Colombia. They were in the middle of a conflict and did not agree on what the solution was or even on what the problem was. They agreed only that the situation they were facing was problematic, and they viewed it as problematic in different respects and for different reasons.

Although the team enjoyed working together and felt some commitment to one another, they were not simply or only one team. They all had stronger connections and commitments to their own organizations and communities (Duque's effort to save Caicedo was the exception that proved this rule). This non-unity was what made their work together so contentious and also so rich and valuable. They collaborated, then, without having a single focus or goal.

Second, the team did not agree on a plan for what should be done in the country. They agreed only that there were four scenarios as to what could happen and that they didn't want the first, status quo, one. Everything else they (and others who made use of the scenarios) did, they worked out as they went along, over the years that followed. So they collaborated without having a single vision or road map.

And third, although the team members held strong views about what ought to happen, they weren't able to compel the others to go along. Here again, the microcosm reflected the macrocosm: the war had gone on so long because no party was able to impose its will on the others. So the team collaborated without being able to change what others were doing.

STRETCH COLLABORATION ABANDONS THE ILLUSION OF CONTROL

Destino Colombia highlights the ways in which our conventional understanding of collaboration is constricted. Stretch collaboration requires us to stretch in three dimensions; in all of these, stretch collaboration includes and goes beyond conventional collaboration (see page 2).

In summary, conventional collaboration assumes that we can control the focus, the goal, the plan to reach this goal, and what each person must do to implement this plan (like a team following a road map). Stretch collaboration, by contrast, offers a way to move forward without being in control (like multiple teams rafting a river).

The first dimension is *how we relate to the people with whom we are collaborating*—our team. In conventional collaboration, we maintain a controlled and constricted focus on achieving

Five Ways to Deal with Problematic Situations

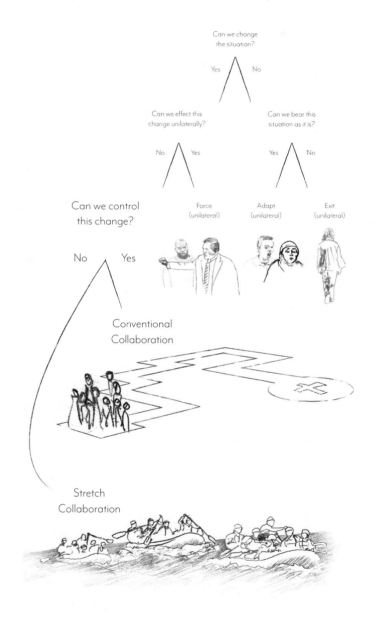

harmony in the team and the good and the objectives of the team as a whole. But in complex and uncontrolled situations, we cannot maintain such a focus because the members of the team have significantly different perspectives, affiliations, and interests, and are free to act on these. So we have to stretch to open up to, embrace, and work with the conflict and connections that exist within and beyond the team.

The second dimension is *how we advance the work of the team*. In conventional collaboration, we focus on reaching clear agreements on the problem we are trying to solve, the best solution to this problem, and the plan to implement this solution, and then on executing this plan as agreed. But in complex, uncontrolled situations, we cannot achieve such definitive agreements or predictable execution, because the team members do not agree with or trust one another and because the results of the team's actions are unpredictable. So we have to stretch to experiment with—try out—multiple perspectives and possibilities in order to discover, one step at a time, what will work and move us forward.

The third dimension is *how we participate—what role we play—in the situation we are trying to address*. In conventional collaboration, we focus on how to get people to change what they are doing so that we can successfully execute our plan. Implicitly we mean getting *other* people to change what they are doing; we see ourselves as outside of or above the situation. But in complex, uncontrolled situations this is simply impossible: we cannot *get* anyone to do anything. So we have to stretch to step fully into the situation and to be open to changing what we ourselves are doing.

To be able to collaborate successfully in complex situations, we must stretch in all three of these dimensions. These stretches are unfamiliar and uncomfortable. The next three chapters lay out how to make these stretches.

5

The First Stretch Is to Embrace
Conflict and Connection

Though it all may be one in the higher eye
Down here where we live it is two.

—Leonard Cohen[1]

*I*n conventional collaboration, we focus on working harmoniously with our team members to achieve what is best for the whole team. We talk rather than fight. This approach works when we are in simple situations that are under control: when all of our perspectives and interests are, or can be made to be, congruent. But when we are in complex, uncontrolled situations where our perspectives and interests are at odds, we need to search out and work with our conflicts as well as our connections. We need to fight as well as talk.

DIALOGUE IS NOT ENOUGH

The most profound experience I have had in collaborating is also the one that raised the most confusing questions. Between 1998 and 2000, I facilitated a project in Guatemala to help implement the peace accords that ended that country's genocidal thirty-six-year civil war. The project brought together leaders of many of the factions that had been caught up in this brutal conflict: cabinet ministers, former army and guerrilla officers, businessmen, indigenous people, journalists, youth. The understandings and relationships and commitments that this project generated produced many important initiatives to repair Guatemala's torn social fabric. United Nations representative Lars Franklin said that this project planted and nurtured many seeds, including four presidential campaigns; contributions to the Commission for Historical Clarification, the Fiscal Agreement Commission, and the Peace Accords Monitoring Commission; work on municipal development strategies, a national antipoverty strategy, and a new university curriculum; and six spin-off national dialogues.[2]

One pivotal event in the work of this team occurred on the final morning of their first workshop. They were sitting in a circle, telling stories about their personal experiences of the war. A man named Ronald Ochaeta, a human rights worker for the Catholic Church, talked about the time he had gone to an indigenous village to witness the exhumation of a mass grave from one of the war's many massacres. Once the earth had been removed, he noticed a number of small bones and asked the forensic scientist if people had had their bones broken during the massacre. The scientist replied that, no, the grave contained the corpses of pregnant women, and the small bones were those of their fetuses.

When Ochaeta finished telling his story, the team was completely silent. I had never experienced a silence like this and was struck dumb. The silence seemed to last five minutes. Then it ended and we carried on with our work.

This episode made a profound impact on the team and on me. When team members were interviewed five years later for a history of the project, many of them traced the important work that they had subsequently done together to the insight and connection manifested in those minutes of silence. One of them said, "After listening to Ochaeta's story, I understood and felt in my heart all that had happened. And there was a feeling that we must struggle to prevent this from happening again." Another said, "In giving his testimony, Ochaeta was sincere, calm, and serene, without a trace of hate in his voice. This gave way to the moment of silence that, I would say, lasted at least one minute. It was horrible! It was a very moving experience for all of us. If you ask any of us, we would say that this moment was like a large communion."[3] In a Catholic country like Guatemala, to refer to a moment of team communion means a moment of a team being one body.

The story of the five minutes of silence in Visión Guatemala became the crowning chapter in my first book, *Solving Tough Problems*. It epitomized my understanding (which originated at Mont Fleur) that connecting with others, and through this revealing and repairing the social whole, was the key to collaboration. The experiences I had with such connecting, in this and other projects, also satisfied my own longing to engage harmoniously with others and with something larger than myself.

In 2008, I went back to Guatemala for the tenth anniversary of the project. I was happy to see my colleagues again but also concerned by what was happening there: a deepening economic crisis; increasingly serious threats from organized crime and elements of the military; and disappointment in the new government, led by our Visión Guatemala teammate, now president, Álvaro Colom. I was interested in what the team thought of the work we had all done together, which I had written about so enthusiastically.

I had lunch with one of my friends, a leftist researcher and activist named Clara Arenas. She knew how significant I had found the dialogue in our team, so she pointedly told me that she and her colleagues had recently become so frustrated with the poor results from the many dialogues that were taking place in Guatemala that they had taken out a full-page newspaper advertisement saying they would no longer participate in these processes. They did this because the government expected that the organizations participating in dialogues would meanwhile desist from organizing strikes and marches and other forms of popular resistance. Arenas and her colleagues were not willing to demobilize—to abandon one of the primary means they had to achieve their objectives. And if they couldn't mobilize to assert their perspectives and positions, then they weren't willing to dialogue to engage with the government. I admired Arenas and knew that she was telling me something important. But I couldn't fit it into the way I understood collaboration, so it stayed with me as an unresolved tension.

Five years later, I had three experiences that showed me how to resolve this tension.

In October 2013, I had a sharp interaction with David Suzuki at a meeting of the board of his foundation in Vancouver. Suzuki is a Canadian geneticist who has presented popular radio and television shows on science for more than forty years. He is an outspoken environmentalist and is among the country's most respected public figures. At that time, he was in the middle of a momentous battle among environmentalists, fossil fuel companies, and the federal government over how Canada should deal with climate change, especially the high carbon dioxide emissions from its oil sands projects.

Before the meeting, I had read one of Suzuki's speeches in which he had said that he would be willing to engage with the CEO of a consortium of oil sands companies only if the CEO would "agree on certain basic things"—for example, that "we are all animals, and as animals our most fundamental need, before anything else, is clean air, clean water, clean soil, clean energy and biodiversity."[4] I thought that Suzuki's insistence that he would dialogue only if the principles he believed in were agreed to in advance was unreasonable and unproductive, and at the meeting I challenged him about this. His position was that given the absence of agreement on such fundamental matters, it was better for him not to engage, so he was instead going to focus his energies on mobilizing public and political opinion in support of the principles he believed in.

This brief exchange struck me. I had heard a similar argument many times from other people in other contexts: that the principles they were asserting were right and needed to be accepted as the starting point for any collaboration. I had always confidently dismissed these arguments on the grounds that such disagreements over principles were usually the reason why collaborations didn't occur, and that agreement could be reached only through—not prior to—engagement and collaboration. But Suzuki's provocation stayed with me, because the principles he was asserting seemed correct and because I held him in such high esteem that I could not easily dismiss his argument.

I could now see that engaging and asserting were complementary rather than opposing ways to make progress on complex challenges, and that both were legitimate and necessary. Different kinds of asserting—debates, campaigns, competitions, rivalries, marches, boycotts, lawsuits, violent confrontations—are part of every story of systemic change. Asserting and counter-asserting inevitably create discord and conflict. But I thought that perhaps some people and organizations could do the asserting while others did the engaging; I had heard activists refer to "outside the room" and "inside the room" roles in efforts to effect change. I hoped that this complementarity meant that others could focus on asserting and I could maintain my comfortable focus on engaging.

In early December 2013, I got home to South Africa, and a few days later Nelson Mandela passed away. For weeks, local and international newspapers were filled with obituaries and reflections on his life and legacy. I also reflected on my understanding of his biography, with which my own had become intertwined. By 2013, social and political relations among South Africans had become more fractious and less forgiving, and many were reevaluating the success of the "miraculous" 1994 transition that Mandela had led.

Now, with this coming right after my exchange with Suzuki, I realized that in focusing so much on Mandela's efforts to achieve

his objectives through engaging and dialoguing with his opponents, I had downplayed his efforts to achieve these same objectives through asserting and fighting. Before Mandela went into
prison, he had led illegal marches and other campaigns against
the apartheid government, gone underground and made clan-
destine trips abroad, and served as the first commander of the
armed guerrilla wing of the African National Congress (as late
as 2007, ANC leaders were still being denied visas to enter the
United States on the grounds that they had been members of
a terrorist organization). After Mandela was released, during
the negotiations leading up the 1994 elections and then during
his presidential term, he often pushed his opponents hard to
advance his positions.

A more complete picture of Mandela's leadership, I could now
see, showed that he knew how and when to engage, and how
and when to assert. The extraordinary transition in South Africa
had been effected through Mandela and others employing both
engaging and asserting. In thinking about my own work, I realized that I had been focusing only on the part of the picture in
which I had been physically present: although I usually met the
people I worked with in workshops designed to enable them to
dialogue with one another, most of them spent a lot of their time
outside the workshops fighting one another. In fact, this fighting
was what made the workshop dialogues so remarkable and useful. So now I wondered whether the engaging and asserting roles
could really, as I had been hoping, be kept separate.

Then, in Thailand in May 2014, after months of violent We
Force confrontations, the army staged its coup. Some of my Thai
colleagues were outraged at this antidemocratic action. Others
were relieved that a further increase in violent conflict had been
halted and hoped that a strict military government could establish a new set of rules that would enable an orderly and peaceful
construction of a We Collaborate scenario.

I wasn't sure which of these positions I agreed with. I understood the limitations and dangers of a military government. And

I also could understand the junta's impulse to impose orderly and peaceful collaboration: they were suppressing asserting to enable engaging.

This extreme event gave me the last piece of the puzzle I had been sitting with. I was surprised by what I could now see: a coup d'état is the logical outcome of the way of collaborating that I had been focused on since Mont Fleur. If we embrace harmonious engaging and reject discordant asserting, then we will end up suffocating the social system we are working with. This is what Arenas had been trying to tell me alll those years earlier in Guatemala.

In stretch collaboration, we cannot only engage and not assert. We need to find a way to do both.

THERE IS MORE THAN ONE WHOLE

One consequence of the imperative to both engage and assert is that prioritizing "the good of the whole"—whether that whole is our team or our organization or our community—is neither sensible nor legitimate.

All social systems consist of multiple wholes that are parts of larger wholes. Author Arthur Koestler coined the term *holon* for something that is simultaneously a whole and a part.[5] For example, a person is a whole in himself or herself; which is part of a team, which is a whole in itself; which is part of an organization, which is a whole; which is part of a sector; and so on. Each of these wholes has its own needs, interests, and ambitions. Each whole can be part of multiple larger wholes.

There is therefore no such thing as "the whole," so to claim to be focusing on achieving "the good of the whole" is misleading if not manipulative: it really means "the good of the whole that matters most to me." If we say that we are prioritizing "the good of the team," for example, then by implication were are deprioritizing the good of individual members of the team (smaller wholes) and of the organization (a larger whole). In stretch collaboration,

The Holonic Structure of Social Systems

we therefore attend not simply to the good of a single whole, but rather to the good of multiple nested and overlapping holons and to the richness and conflict that this inevitably reveals.

In facilitating collaborative teams, I have made this mistake by focusing on the objectives of the team as a whole and thereby implicitly asking participants to leave their individual and organizational objectives at the door. In doing this, I was also conveniently overlooking the fact that the interests of these larger and smaller wholes were identical only for me and perhaps the team leader: we were the only ones who, when we championed the interests of the whole team, were at the same time championing our own interests.

In 2013, almost thirty years after I left Montreal, I moved back there with my wife, Dorothy, to open the Canadian office of Reos Partners. This gave me the opportunity to see my home with fresh eyes. I found this experience delightful and also puzzling: after many years living in other places, I noticed something distinctive in the low-key way that many of the Canadians I worked with approached the challenges we were dealing with, but I didn't know what to make of it.

The following year, in connection with the upcoming 150th anniversary of Canada's founding, my colleagues and I conducted interviews with fifty Canadian leaders. We asked each of them what he or she thought it would take for Canadians to succeed in creating a good future.[6]

During the period when we were conducting interviews, acrimonious and disturbing debates were taking place in Canada and internationally about the place of Muslims in Western societies. One of the people I interviewed was Jean Charest, a former premier of Quebec, who made a striking comment about the political incentives for enemyfying which foreshadowed the US presidential contest two years later:

> Demagogues thrive by cultivating insecurity and demonizing certain groups. They emphasize differences rather than the things we have in common. Human

nature is such that we remember negatives better than positives. It's easier to vote against something—or someone—than for it. For politicians, it's always tempting to pit one group against the other because it works so well and so rapidly.

Then I interviewed Khalil Shariff, the CEO of the Aga Khan Foundation Canada, an organization established by the worldwide spiritual leader of the Shia Ismaili Muslims. Shariff had a thoughtful perspective on Canadian culture that I had never heard before:

> In the world as a whole, the notion of homogeneity is quickly disappearing, for two reasons. First, we're more aware of our individual differences—our "selfness"— than ever before. Second, we have experienced demographic movements that historically were unheard of. These two factors mean that the idea of managing difference and being able to live in some kind of common framework might be fundamental for any society today.
>
> Someone once told me that, for an individual, humility is the king of virtues. What is the king of virtues for a society—the virtue from which all other virtues and capacities stem? I wonder if the capacity for pluralism might be the source from which all others stem.
>
> If you can build the social capacity to deal with pluralism, then you can deal with a host of other questions. The scaffolding of Canadian society—this commitment to pluralism—is invisible to most Canadians. We don't always understand it explicitly, and we might take it for granted, but it is embedded in us.

Shariff also offered me a personal challenge: "Perhaps this collaborative work you have been doing around the world, which you are so proud of, is not simply an expression of your personal gifts. Perhaps you have been expressing something of the culture you were brought up in." Canadian culture is not the only one that values pluralism, and Canadians often also express contrary values—for example, in their brutal suppression of indigenous culture. But Shariff was pointing out the crucial value of a culture of pluralism to being able to live and work with contradictory and confounding wholes.

EVERY HOLON HAS TWO DRIVES

The key to being able to work with multiple wholes is being able to work with both power and love. I proposed this framing in my 2010 book *Power and Love* and continue to find it crucial to making sense of the dynamics of collaboration.

In this book I defined power, following the insightful work of theologian Paul Tillich, as "the drive of everything living to realize itself."[7] The drive of power is manifested in the behavior of asserting. In groups, the power drive produces differentiation (the development of a variety of forms and functions) and individuation (parts operating separately from one another).[8]

I defined love, also following Tillich, as "the drive towards the unity of the separated." The drive of love is manifested in the behavior of engaging. In groups, the love drive produces homogenization (the sharing of information and capability) and integration (parts connecting into a whole).

My thesis was that every person and group possesses both of these drives and that it is always a mistake to employ only one. Love and power are not options that we can choose between; they are complementary poles and we must choose both. Here I was elaborating on the point that Martin Luther King Jr., a student of Tillich, made when he said, "Power without love is reckless and abusive, and love without power is sentimental and anemic."[9] I cited many examples in small and large social systems of the twin degeneracies that occur when one of these drives is exercised without the other, and of the generative synthesis that occurs only when they are exercised together.

Every living whole or holon has the drives of love and power. Love, the drive toward unity, reflects a holon's partness: that it is part of larger wholes. Power, the drive toward self-realization, reflects its wholeness: that it is a whole in itself. Being able to work with both love and power is therefore a prerequisite to being able to work with multiple wholes.

I once talked about this book to a Dutch association of interim managers. These are professionals who do a variety of management jobs, filling temporary gaps in organizations that have special projects or someone on leave or a delay in a new manager taking up his or her position. Their reaction to my thesis was that the need to work with both power and love was obvious: that their whole job as managers was reconciling the drive to self-realization of individual team members with the need to unite the team to achieve its collective self-realization.

I also developed a better understanding of the centrality of power and love for working with social systems as I spent more time with politicians and activists. I was surprised when Antonio Aranibar, who managed a political analysis unit at the United Nations, sponsored the Spanish edition of this book. When I asked him why he thought the book was useful, he said that in his view the essence of politics is aligning the interests of smaller and larger wholes.

Then Betty Sue Flowers suggested that I study how US President Lyndon Johnson had done this aligning. I found a biography of Johnson that contains a riveting account of how he succeeded in enacting landmark civil rights legislation through attending carefully to the interests of individual legislators and thereby harnessing their individual political wholes into a collective one. The biographer writes about a meeting between Johnson and historian Arthur Schlesinger:

Johnson turned to the individual senators, the other forty-eight Democratic senators. "I want you to know the kind of material I have to work with," he said. Schlesinger was to recall that "he didn't do all of them, but he did most of them"—in a performance the historian was never to forget. Senator by senator Johnson ran down the list: each man's strengths and weaknesses, who liked liquor too much, and who liked women, and how he had to know when to reach a senator at his own home and when at his mistress's, who was controlled by the big power company in his state, and who listened to the public electrification cooperatives, who responded to the union pleas and who to the agricultural lobby instead, and which senator responded to one argument and which senator to the opposite argument. He did brief, but brilliant, imitations; "When he came to Chavez, whose trouble was alcoholism, Johnson imitated Chavez drunk—very funny."[10]

Alternate power and love

After I published *Power and Love*, I learned that psychologist Barry Johnson had developed a methodology for mapping the relationship between poles such as power and love. Johnson suggests that we must differentiate between problems that can be solved and polarities that cannot be solved but only managed.[11] He explains that in a polarity the relationship between two poles is analogous to the relationship between inhaling and exhaling. We cannot choose between inhaling and exhaling: if we only inhaled, we would die of too much carbon dioxide, and if we only exhaled, we would die of too little oxygen. Instead, we must both inhale and exhale, not at the same time but alternately. First we inhale to get oxygen into our blood; then when our cells convert oxygen to carbon dioxide and the carbon dioxide builds up in our blood, we exhale to let it out; then when the oxygen in our blood falls too low, we inhale; and so on. If we are healthy, this involuntary physiological feedback system maintains the necessary alternation between inhaling and exhaling and enables us to live and grow.

Barry Johnson's mapping enabled me to make sense of my confusing experiences with engaging and asserting. It explained what we need to do to exercise love and power and to work with multiple wholes. I could now see that my early understanding of collaboration—that it meant embracing harmony and rejecting discord—limited its applicability and effectiveness. When I tried to employ this kind of harmony-only collaboration, I usually failed and therefore ended up defaulting to adapting, forcing, or exiting.

When we collaborate, we exercise love and power alternately. First we engage with others. As our engaging continues and intensifies, eventually it produces in them an uncomfortable feeling of fusing and capitulating: of having to subordinate or compromise what matters to them in order to maintain the engagement. This reaction or feeling of discomfort is a signal that they need to switch to asserting or pushing for what matters to them (as Arenas and Suzuki did). But then, as their asserting continues and intensifies, eventually it produces in us an impulse to block or push back or resist. This reaction or feeling is a signal that we need to return to engaging. (In this simple example, I have given each party only one role, but in fact both parties can play both roles.)

We can understand the imperative to alternate between engaging and asserting if we consider what happens if either of these two reactions or edges of discomfort is ignored and overstepped. If we keep asserting and pushing past the other's attempts to resist, then the result will be our forcing or imposing what matters to us onto them, and thereby defeating or crushing them. In the extreme case, then, employing only asserting produces war

Managing the Polarity of Love and Power

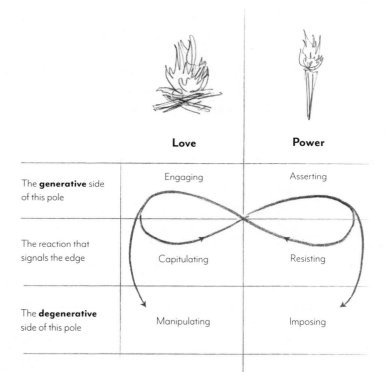

	Love	**Power**
The **generative** side of this pole	Engaging	Asserting
The reaction that signals the edge	Capitulating	Resisting
The **degenerative** side of this pole	Manipulating	Imposing

and death (this was the possibility of a civil war that some Thais feared during the violent clashes of 2013–2014). This risk, which is widely recognized, is why it is important to notice the feeling of resistance that signals that asserting is going too far and that engaging is required. Engaging when it is needed prevents asserting from becoming degenerative.

On the other hand, if we keep engaging others beyond the point where they feel they are being compromised, then the result will be our manipulating or disempowering them. In the extreme case, then, employing only engaging produces suffocation: the kind of lifelessness that is produced through imposed peace or pacification (this was the possibility of deadening that some Thais feared would be the outcome of the 2014 coup). This risk, which is less recognized, is why it is important to notice the feeling of capitulating that signals that engaging is going too far and that asserting is required. Asserting when it is needed prevents engaging from becoming degenerative.

This less recognized risk of unconstrained engaging is what I had been missing in my post–Mont Fleur embrace of engaging and dialoguing, and rejection of asserting and fighting. Barry Johnson points out that if we are focused above all on the risk of unconstrained asserting (as I was), then we will mistakenly understand engaging to be an ideal rather than only a pole, and thereby produce this opposite pitfall. The mistake I was making was to reject asserting as uncivilized and dangerous, and therefore to push it into the shadows. This didn't make the asserting disappear; it just drove it underground so that I exercised it less consciously and cleanly.

Psychologist James Hillman points out that many people who, like me, work in "helping professions" make this mistake of rejecting asserting and power. He writes,

> Why are the conflicts about power so ruthless—less so in business and politics, where they are an everyday matter, than in the idealistic professions of clergy, med-

icine, the arts, teaching and nursing? In business and politics, it seems, there is less idealism and more sense of shadow. Power is not repressed but lived with as a daily companion; moreover, it is not declared to be the enemy of love. So long as the notion of power is itself corrupted by a romantic opposition with love, power will indeed corrupt. The corruption begins not in power, but in the ignorance about it.[12]

When we block asserting, we pervert it and make it degenerative and dangerous.

As Hillman points out, in business and politics the value of asserting (competition and contestation) is commonly accepted, as is the coexistence of asserting and engaging (for example, cooperating to maintain a playing field on which fair competition can take place). But in the field of collaboration, the conventional misunderstanding that you need to engage rather than assert implies that we need to make deliberate efforts to enable generative asserting.

Conventional collaboration focuses on engaging, and that does not make room for asserting, so it becomes ossified and brittle; it settles into a stupor and gets stuck. Stretch collaboration, by contrast, cycles generatively between engaging and asserting, enabling a social system—a family, an organization, a country—to evolve to higher levels.[13]

When I have given lectures about *Power and Love*, I have observed that most people are more comfortable either with love and engaging, or with power and asserting. Their preferences are both personal and cultural. They may be able, when they are in low-stress contexts (such as with colleagues and friends), to fluidly employ both of these drives, but when they are in high-stress contexts (such as with opponents and enemies), they default to and get stuck in their comfort zone. Often they recognize the danger of overutilizing their stronger drive and hold back. Some people have said to me, "At work, I feel more comfortable exercising power—I see love as something for home—but as a result, I am often accused of bullying, so I try to rein in my power." Other people have said, "I feel more comfortable exercising love—I see power as dangerous—but as a result, I often get hurt, so I try to limit my love." Moreover, often people choose to focus on employing their stronger drive, and they let someone else—their spouse, their business partner, another part of their organization—employ the other one.

Stretch collaboration requires all of us to embrace both love and power. If we constrict—if we weaken our stronger pole or outsource our weaker pole—we will not be successful in collaborating in tough contexts. So we need to do the opposite: practice employing our weaker pole and thereby strengthen it. We need to stretch.

The key to alternating between engaging and asserting is to know when to employ which, so as to keep the cycle generative rather than degenerative. David Culver, the former CEO of Alcan, the Canadian aluminum company, was known as an outstanding manager. When he retired, social innovation researcher Frances Westley asked him for his secret. He answered, "When I feel myself wanting to be compassionate, I try to be tough, and when I feel myself wanting to be tough, I try to be compassionate." So moving between engaging and asserting requires paying attention to the feedback that signals imbalance (crossing the edge into degeneracy) and then making the corresponding rebalancing move. When our engaging is producing capitulation and therefore at risk of manipulating, it is time to foster asserting. When our asserting is producing resistance and therefore at risk of forcing, it time to foster engaging. The key is not to maintain a position of static balance but to notice and correct dynamic imbalance.

The skill to employing both engaging and asserting is to be alert and courageous enough to be able to make a countervailing move when it is required. In a situation or system that is dominated by engaging, if we begin to assert, then we may be seen as

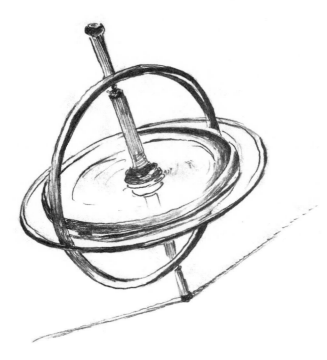

balance in movement
movement in balance

impolite or aggressive. In a situation or system dominated by asserting, if we begin to engage, then we may be seen as weak or disloyal. Going against the tide therefore takes patience: to be able to wait for the moment when the dominant movement is producing frustration, doubt, or fear, and then to make the countervailing move.

The essential practice required for embracing conflict and connection is, then, to attend to how we are employing love and power. When we notice ourselves overemploying love—insisting that the unity and good of the collective whole that we care about must be paramount—then we need to employ power and to live with the conflict, perhaps disturbing, that this will produce. And when we notice ourselves overemploying power—insisting that the expression and interests of the constituent part that we care about must be paramount—then we need to employ love and to live with the collectivism, perhaps constraining, that this will produce. We must keep employing both.

6

The Second Stretch Is to Experiment a Way Forward

Walker, there is no path. The path is made by walking.

—Antonio Machado[1]

*I*n conventional collaboration, we move forward by agreeing on the problem, the solution, and the plan to implement the solution, and then executing this plan. This approach works when we are in simple situations that are under control: when we can get such agreement among our collaborators and also get our plan to produce the results we intend. But when we are in complex, uncontrolled situations, we need to experiment with different possible articulations and actions: we need to take a step forward, observe what happens, and then take another step.

WE CANNOT CONTROL THE FUTURE, BUT WE CAN INFLUENCE IT

I see my work as helping people collaborate to address their most important challenges, so I am not usually active in choosing what challenges to address. But some years ago, through my experiences in Colombia and Guatemala and elsewhere, I became concerned about the widespread problems associated with illegal drugs such as heroin, cocaine, and methamphetamine. Then in 2012 I unexpectedly discovered an opening to do something about my concern.

Later, once I had started to work on this issue, I was struck by the extent to which governments around the world had been attempting to implement one single strategy for forty years: waging a "war on drugs" through criminalizing the production, sale, and consumption of certain specified substances. Drug control officials enforced a strict set of global, national, and local laws at a cost of more than $100 billion per year.[2] In official policy debates, they excluded discussion of any alternatives to this strategy. And yet in spite of this singularly focused investment of resources, drug-related addiction, criminality, corruption, incarceration, and violence all remained high.

In the 1990s, some political leaders started to question this established strategy. One of the most outspoken of these was Colombian President Juan Manuel Santos. In November 2011, he said, "On this issue we sometimes feel that the world is pedaling on a stationary bicycle. We keep fighting against drugs, but the drugs continue to flow."[3] He repeated this point many times in many meetings, declaring that he was searching for a way for drug policy to get unstuck and move forward.

My colleagues Joaquin Moreno and Gustavo Mutis and I had worked with Santos on Destino Colombia and other projects since 1996. Then in February 2012, when the four of us were briefly together in Bogotá for the launch of the Spanish edition of *Power and Love*, we conceived a project modeled on Destino Colombia to bring together international leaders to explore new options for drug policy. In April 2012, Santos proposed this project to a summit of all the presidents and prime ministers of the Americas. They agreed and assigned the work to the Organization of American States (OAS) in Washington, DC. I was delighted to see what was possible when I actively stepped into an opportunity to make a difference.

This is how, from May 2012 to May 2013, I ended up working with my colleagues and the OAS on an ambitious effort to articulate alternatives to the war on drugs.[4] The secretary general of the OAS, José Miguel Insulza, was pleased to have received this important mandate but surprised to find that my colleagues and I were also supposed to be involved. The OAS's usual approach to achieving its mandates was to seek agreements through formal, rationalistic, diplomatic negotiations among its member governments, and many observers were skeptical about whether such an approach would enable it to make a difference on such a difficult, stuck issue. By contrast, my colleagues and I wanted to produce options through an informal creative collaboration among diverse governmental and nongovernmental stakeholders.

Because of these differences between the OAS's and our standing and approach, our first meeting with Insulza and his team overflowed with suspicion and conflict. Both they and we wanted to be in control of the project, but because of the way it had been established, neither of us could. So in order to implement this collaborative project, we ourselves had to collaborate.

We needed to work out how to organize the project, which stakeholders to involve, and how to connect to official governmental processes. We had a common interest in the success of this high-stakes and high-profile project, but also different views on and interests in all of these matters. So this was the beginning of a full year of daily engaging and asserting; friendly conversations and angry arguments; cooperation and competition. I found this whole experience, of working on a project that was so important to me with people I did not see eye to eye with, to be both exhilarating and exasperating.

We agreed to establish a working team of forty-six leaders from across all the countries of the Americas and the sectors involved in drug policy: politics, security, business, health, education, indigenous cultures, international organizations, the justice system, and civil society. This team met for two three-day workshops in Panama City in January and February of 2013. Their primary task was to agree on a set of scenarios about what could—not what would or what should—happen in and around the drug problem. This framing was crucial because it enabled the members of the team, who had radically different and entrenched positions on the problem and the solution, to shift their conversation from a usual rigid one about whose position was right to an unusual fluid one about what was possible.

My colleagues and I focused on organizing the project to enable the team to connect and think and act freely and afresh. The workshops included a variety of activities that were not usual in OAS meetings: visits to a clinic and police station and the canal and other local sites to observe firsthand different aspects of this complex situation; sharing personal histories of working on the drug problem; and session after session of creative and structured team conversations about what was happening and could happen.

Out of these sessions the team created a set of scenarios. No topics were prescribed or proscribed. During the conversations in the workshops and the subsequent drafting of the team's report, every member of the team was given an equal opportunity to contribute, and none of their contributions were given greater weight than others. Betty Sue Flowers, the editor of the report, patiently took account of every input, iterating and circulating tens of drafts. And without precedent for such a politically sensitive undertaking, Insulza committed to the team that he would publish their report as they wrote it, rather than as the OAS or member governments wanted it written.

The central tension within the team was between the government officials who were trying to make current drug policy work and the nongovernmental activists who were trying to reform it. Their positions were not symmetrical: the officials had more formal power and responsibility and felt more defensive of the status quo. Neither side trusted the other. During the first workshop, one official told me that he thought the reformers were smoking marijuana in a hallway, and I thought I smelled it, too. Later I realized that the accusation was not only untrue but ridiculous. I was amazed that I had become so involved in this work and had taken on board so much of the mutual mistrust that I was even able to smell a nonexistent odor.

We had carefully organized the project so that the team could work out its conclusions freely, transparently, and democratically, and after weeks of vigorous arguments this approach paid off. Through many conversations in the workshops and on email and conference calls, the team agreed on the text of their report. It discussed several alternative futures where governments departed radically from the war on drugs, including scenarios of some countries' ignoring the international treaties and allowing drug traffickers free passage through their territory; of health-based rather than security-based policies; and of experimentation with new ways of regulating drugs, such as decriminalization, depenalization, and legalization.

Insulza then sent the report to Santos and the other government leaders as written. It was the first time that an officially mandated document had discussed possible strategies for dealing with drugs other than the established one. Contrary to the expectations of the skeptics, the OAS had permitted an uncontrolled process, and the results were innovative and important.

When Santos launched the report, he said, "The four scenarios are not recommendations of what should happen or forecasts of what will happen; they simply provide us with realistic options, without prejudices or dogmas."[5] Sixteen months later, Insulza reflected, "The report had a huge, immediate impact. It managed to open up a discussion as frank as it was unprecedented of all the options available. It has set a 'before' and an 'after' in our way of addressing the drug phenomenon."[6]

After the challenging year I spent working on this project, I was thrilled with our collective achievement. I was also furious that I had had to push so hard to get my OAS counterparts to go along with the way of working that I had been advocating: involving all actors, including opponents and enemies; engaging this team in a creative process; and giving them control of the text. Once I calmed down, however, I could see that I was angry at them for the same behavior that I myself was exhibiting: doing everything in my power to have things be the way I wanted them to be. I was learning to stretch toward full-strength engagement and assertion.

This project did not solve the problem of drugs in the Americas. It did not produce a new policy or plan of action. What it did do was produce a set of radically new shared narratives of alternative possible futures (the four scenarios) and important new working relationships among the protagonists (especially between the officials and the reformers). Along with other developments in the drug policy world that occurred during that year, especially marijuana legalization in Uruguay and in some states in the US, we opened up new possibilities for the future of drug policy in the Americas and beyond, including greater openness to hitherto off-limits options, such as experimentation with alternative models for regulating demand and supply, practices for reducing the harms of consumption, reforms of prison sentencing, and revisions to the global treaties. The project helped this hemispheric social system, which had been stuck for forty years, to get unstuck and move forward.

This project gave me a clear picture of what it takes to influence a situation that we cannot control. The situation we were dealing with was out of control on at least three levels: the production and consumption of a multitude of old and new drugs by a multitude of legal and illegal actors could not controlled; the views and positions on drug policy of governmental and nongovernmental stakeholders from around the world could not be controlled; and the outputs of our collaborative process among the independent project participants could not be controlled.

Once the project team gave up on trying to control this situation, however, we were more able to make progress on dealing with it. It turned out that not only was it not possible for the participants to agree on either the problem or the solution, but also it was not necessary, and this realization liberated us to make our way forward without agreement. This robust collaboration in our staff and stakeholder teams produced new possibilities for the situation we were trying to deal with. The most important of these new possibilities was a readiness to go beyond the rigid enforcement of one established strategy and to start to experiment fluidly with different new strategies.

WE ARE CROSSING THE RIVER BY FEELING FOR STONES

In stretch collaboration, we cocreate our way forward. We cannot know our route before we set out; we cannot predict or control it; we can only discover it along the way. Working in this manner can be both exciting and unnerving.

The participants in stretch collaborations often do not agree with or like or trust one another enough to be willing to commit to any plan of action other than one that is modest, short-term, and low risk. Given that they are participating in the collaboration voluntarily and provisionally, with no one having control over the others, they almost always have the option of exiting. Collaborators do what they want to do, so attempts to force or cajole them into doing otherwise don't work. All of us involved in the drug project stayed with it through its ups and downs because we thought that it offered us an important opportunity to do something about an issue that was important to us.

Management professor Peter Senge says, "Most leadership strategies are doomed to failure from the outset. Leaders instigating change are often like gardeners standing over their plants, imploring them: 'Grow! Try harder! You can do it!' No gardener tries to convince a plant to 'want' to grow: if the seed does not have the potential to grow, there's nothing anyone can do to make a difference."[7] Stretch collaboration is like gardening: we can create some of the conditions for a collective effort to flourish, but we cannot direct it to do so.

Even when collaborators are willing to commit to a plan of action, these commitments and plans usually produce only the beginning and not the end of a process of change. In a complex and contentious context, the only way we can know if a plan will work—if the parties will take the actions they have committed to, and if these actions will have the intended impacts—is to try it. It is arrogant and unrealistic to assume that our idea will work as planned. In these contexts, the only sensible way to move forward is to take one step at a time and learn as we go.

Stretch collaboration therefore involves more than making a deal or an agreement. It is an ongoing and emergent process in which it is more important to act than to agree. What is crucial is to create the conditions under which participants can act freely and creatively, and in doing so create a path forward. Success in collaborating does not mean that the participants agree with or like or trust one another: maybe they will and maybe they won't. Success means that they are able to get unstuck and take a next step.

Stretch collaboration also involves more than formulating, agreeing, and executing a plan. It can be a useful discipline to create a plan—as long as we hold it lightly and change it when it no longer makes sense. Stretch collaboration involves making our way forward amid uncertainty and contestation. Deng Xiaoping, former leader of the Chinese Communist Party, used a memorable image to describe taking such an approach to China's transition toward a socialist market economy: "We are crossing the river by feeling for stones."[8]

The principle that teams need to feel, more than plan, their way forward is well established in the management literature. Organizational theorist Karl Weick tells a story, perhaps apocryphal, about a group of soldiers on military maneuvers in Switzerland:

The young lieutenant of a small Hungarian detachment in the Alps sent a reconnaissance unit into the icy wilderness. It began to snow immediately, snowed for two days, and the unit did not return. The lieutenant suffered, fearing that he had dispatched his own people to death. But the third day the unit came back. Where had they been? How had they made their way? Yes, they said, we considered ourselves lost and waited for the end. And then one of us found a map in his pocket. That calmed us down. We pitched camp, lasted out the snowstorm, and then with the map we discovered our bearings. And here we are. The lieutenant borrowed this remarkable map and had a good look at it. He discovered to his astonishment that it was not a map of the Alps, but a map of the Pyrenees.[9]

Weick's thesis is that people find their way forward not necessarily because they have a good map or plan. Instead it is because they "begin to act, they generate tangible outcomes in some context, and this helps them discover what is occurring, what needs to be explained, and what should be done next." They don't need to have a clear vision or goal; they only need to have some shared sense of the challenge or problematic situation they are trying to overcome (in the case of the soldiers it was to get back to base). Collaborative teams typically make progress not by carefully executing an excellent plan to achieve agreed objectives, but by acting and learning from this acting. When things go well, they do this (like the soldiers) with hope, alertness, energy, flexibility, and mutual support.

Management professor Henry Mintzberg develops this principle further. He points out that there are two opposite ways to realize a strategy: with a deliberate strategy that succeeds in realizing an intention, or with an emergent strategy that is realized despite or in the absence of an intention. He observes that in organizations, few managers actually can or do implement purely deliberate strategies:

Types of Strategy

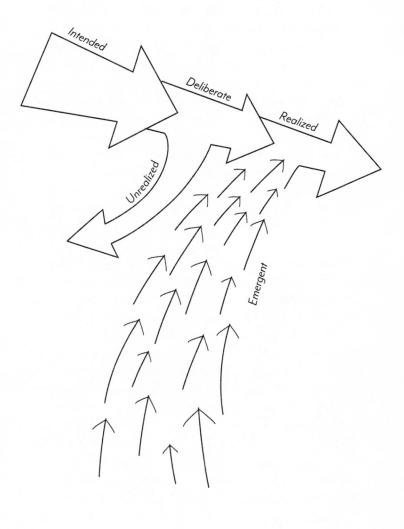

For a strategy to be perfectly deliberate—that is, for the realized strategy (a pattern of actions) to form exactly as intended—at least three conditions would seem to have to be satisfied. First, there must have existed precise intentions in the organization, articulated in a relatively concrete level of detail, so that there can be no doubt about what was desired before any actions were taken. Secondly, because organization means collective action, to dispel any possible doubt about whether or not the intentions were organizational, they must have been common to virtually all the actors: either shared as their own or else accepted from leaders, probably in response to some sort of controls. Thirdly, these collective intentions must have been realized exactly as intended, which means that no external force (market, technological, political, etc.) could have interfered with them. The environment, in other words, must have been either perfectly predictable, totally benign, or else under the full control of the organization. These three conditions constitute a tall order, so that we are unlikely to find any perfectly deliberate strategies in organizations.[10]

If within a simple organizational situation these conditions are rarely met, then within a complex and conflictual multiorganization situation they are never met. In stretch collaboration, therefore, we advance through processes that are primarily emergent rather than deliberate.

We realize emergent strategies by experimenting. We try out ideas that we think might work and then learn from the results, using design-based methodologies such as rapid prototyping. We articulate and test our assumptions, trying to discover errors early on, when they are smaller and it is less costly to fix them ("fail early, fail forward"). We understand that making a mistake is a success rather than a failure; the failure would be not acting and therefore not learning, or delaying acting and therefore making larger and costlier mistakes. In the drugs project, we worked in this way in the team's many small iterations of their report, in the articulation of multiple possible scenarios rather than one recommended policy, and in the introduction of one scenario focused on policy experimentation.

CREATIVITY REQUIRES NEGATIVE CAPABILITY

The process of experimenting is a process of creating. My colleague, artist Jeff Barnum, pointed this principle out to me by showing me a film made from time-lapse photographs of Pablo Picasso creating a painting of a matador.[11] Picasso starts out by making a few rough marks on the canvas and then adds detail and color. He changes and paints over what he has done, again and again. At one point he obliterates a beautifully rendered bull's head that is right in the center of the piece. Barnum explains:

> The creative process is a process of finding, not of projecting something already seen and known in one's mind. Artists do not manifest an already-finished mental picture; they hunt in a distinct medium, within the limits of its inherent properties, for an arrangement of that medium that accords with an inspiration. We see Picasso destroy as willingly as he creates. One has to be willing to let go in a kind of fierce way—to fiercely overcome any tendency to hold on to cherished parts at the expense of the emergence of the whole. Picasso is not after a beautiful face or a wonderful hand: he's after a whole composition that conveys specific ideas and feelings. He finds the form that serves the function. The needed inner gestures here are fearlessness in letting go of what isn't working and boldness in proposing new solutions.

Barnum and I connected this principle with Otto Scharmer's "Theory U."[12] The U shape refers to the movement from sensing to presencing (discussed later in the chapter) to creating: this movement does not follow a straight, direct route. Barnum points out that at the outset of this process, we cannot yet see what we will create; it is around the corner of the bottom of the U. We have an idea of what we are trying to accomplish but not of how to get there. The word *creativity* is used so loosely that we often forget its essential meaning: to bring forth something that does not yet exist. The drug project brought forth an official international policy debate that did not yet exist.

The discipline required to discover a way forward creatively is to try something out, step back and look at the result, and then change it, iterating over and over. I learned this discipline through writing books, where even if I spend months thinking about and outlining what I want to say, it is only when I write it out and look at what I have written that I can know what makes sense and what I need to rewrite and to write next. I can produce a good text only by reworking a bad text a hundred times.

Working in this way requires being able to look at a still-inadequate and still-incomplete result without becoming frightened ("I am a failure!") or attached ("This *must* be right!"). We need to be present to what is actually happening rather than what we wish would happen. We need to be able to maintain our equanimity in a conflictual, uncomfortable situation where we don't know how things will turn out, or when, or even if we will succeed. The poet John Keats called this "negative capability," which he defined as "being capable of being in uncertainties, mysteries, and doubts without any irritable reaching after fact and reason."[13] I have had to stretch to go beyond the plan-agree-implement model I was trained in toward becoming comfortable with staying "in uncertainties, mysteries, and doubts" and feeling my way forward.

One of the reasons why stretch collaboration is so daunting is that it requires us to undertake this kind of patient and relaxed experimentation and iteration—and to do so not only privately, like a painter or poet, but together with our opponents and enemies, on issues that really matter to us, risking having our mistakes exposed publicly.

LISTEN FOR POSSIBILITY RATHER THAN FOR CERTAINTY

The members of the drug project team were able together to imagine, articulate, and make possible new policy options because they were able to listen to one another openly. Open listening is the key practice required to experiment a way forward.

Open listening enables us to discover options that are not yet apparent. It means cultivating the capacity to notice afresh. Buddhist teacher Shunryu Suzuki says, "In the beginner's mind, there are many possibilities, but in the expert's mind there are few."[14]

When I was writing *Solving Tough Problems: An Open Way of Talking, Listening, and Creating New Realities*, Betty Sue Flowers said to me, "I am pleased that you are writing about different ways of listening. Most people don't realize that there is more than one kind of listening, just as they don't realize that there is more than one kind of woman." We are used to making distinctions in the creative, masculine function, but not in the receptive, feminine one. The key way to increase the creativity of a collaboration is to open up the listening of the collaborators.

The clearest example of such a shift to creative listening in my own experience is in the work of the 1998–2000 Visión Guatemala team. The major contribution that team made to helping their country advance after the genocide was not the scenario stories they agreed to tell, or any single vision or plan they came up with. It was the way in which many members of this heterogeneous group, including former combatants, succeeded in making their way forward together over the years that followed, in different configurations, on a range of important initiatives. They were able to do this because they had shifted the way they related to one another—and specifically the way they listened.

Scholar Katrin Käufer led a group of researchers who interviewed members of this team about their experiences of working together.[15] She identified an evolution in the way the team talked and listened that accorded with a model that her colleague Otto Scharmer was in the process of developing.[16] This model posits that there are four distinct ways in which we can talk and listen that are differentiated by the place from which we are operating. These four ways differ according to whether they give priority to one whole or to multiple parts, and to whether they reenact existing realities or enact new ones. We employ these four ways, sometimes intentionally and sometimes habitually, in different settings and sequences.

At the beginning of the first workshop of the Visión Guatemala team, they were deeply mistrustful of one another and reluctant to engage. Project director Elena Díez Pinto recalled:

> When I arrived at the hotel for lunch before the start of the initial meeting, the first thing I noticed was that the indigenous people were sitting together. The military guys were sitting together. The human rights group was sitting together. I thought, "They are not going to speak to each other." In Guatemala, we have learned to be very polite. We are so polite that we say "Yes" but think "No." I was worried that we would be so polite that the real issues would never emerge.

This is the first way of talking and listening, which Scharmer calls *downloading*. Here I listen from within myself and my story. I am deaf to other stories; I hear only what confirms my own story ("I knew that already"). The talking associated with downloading is telling: I say what I always say, because I think that my story is either the only true one or the only one that is safe or polite to tell. I assert that there is only one whole (for example, one objective or team or strategy) and ignore or suppress others. Downloading is the typical behavior of experts, fundamentalists,

Four Ways of Talking and Listening

Enacting new realities

Presencing

"What I am noticing here and now is..."

Primacy of the
whole

Dialoguing

"In my experience..."

Primacy of the
parts

"The truth is..."
Downloading

"In my opinion..."
Debating

Reenacting existing realities

dictators, and people who are arrogant or angry or afraid. Stretch collaborations among people who don't agree with or like or trust one another always start in downloading mode ("The truth is . . .").

Later during that first Visión Guatemala workshop, the team expressed their different views of what had been going on in the country. As team member Gonzalo de Villa recalled,

> The first round in the first session was extremely negative because we were all looking back to the events of recent years, which had left a deep imprint on us. A first moment full of pessimism was generated. Suddenly, a young man stood up and questioned our pessimism in a very direct manner. This moment marked the beginning of an important change, and we continually referred to it afterwards. That a young man would suddenly call us "old pessimists" was an important contribution.

This second way of talking and listening is *debating*. Here I listen from the outside, factually and objectively, like a judge in a debate or a courtroom ("This is correct and that is incorrect"). The talking associated with debating is a clash of ideas: each person says what he or she thinks, and some ideas and people win and others lose. This mode is more open than downloading because people are now expressing their different views and are aware that these are their views and not the truth ("In my opinion . . .").

During the Visión Guatemala team's second workshop, they engaged in a difficult conversation about what had happened during the civil war. Julio Balconi, a retired army general, struggled to get the others to understand why he had done what he had during the war, which was a perspective that most of the others were not sympathetic to. Raquel Zelaya, the cabinet secretary of peace charged with overseeing the implementation of the Peace Accords, leaned over to him and said gently, "I know that nobody enrolls in the military academy in order to learn how to massacre women and children."

This third kind of talking and listening is *dialoguing*. Here I listen to others as if from inside them, empathetically and subjectively ("I hear where you are coming from"). The talking associated with dialoguing is self-reflective ("In my experience . . ."). This mode opens up new possibilities because now we are working with multiple living holons, each expressing its power and love.

In the previous chapter, I wrote about the time in the Visión Guatemala workshop when Ronald Ochaeta told the story of having witnessed the exhumation of a mass grave, which was followed by the five minutes of silence in the team. This was the incident that many members of the team later referred to and that one said was "like a large communion."

This fourth way of talking and listening is *presencing*; this neologism combines pre-sensing (sensing what is in the process of coming into being) and being fully present.[17] Here I listen not from within myself or another, paying attention just to one specific idea or person, but from the larger system ("What I am noticing here and now is . . ."). When I am in a group that is presencing, it is as if the boundaries between people have disappeared, so that when one person talks, he or she is articulating something for the whole group or system, and when I listen, it is as if to the whole group or system. Ochaeta was not a core member of the Visión Guatemala team, and although he told the story, the team did not really hear it as *his* story. They heard it as an expression of a crucial aspect of the Guatemalan reality that they needed to pay attention to and act on.

Díez Pinto and I talked at length about the significance of this five minutes of silence. She quoted a phrase from the *Popol Vuh*, the local sacred book of the K'iche' people: "We did not put our ideas together. We put our purposes together. And we agreed, and then we decided." She and I thought that Ochaeta's story had enabled the team to go beyond their individual ideas and experiences to discover their shared purpose, and that this purpose enabled them to work together over the years that followed, notwithstanding their differences. Presencing is a shared sense of the potential of a whole that includes and transcends our individual wholes.

All four of these modes of talking and listening are legitimate and useful. It's not that we need to employ only one mode, but rather that we need to be able to move fluently and fluidly among them. And if we spend all of our time downloading and debating, then we will only reenact existing realities: we will continue to think what we have been thinking and do what we have been doing. If we want to cocreate new realities, then we need to be able to spend at least some of our time dialoguing and presencing.

7

The Third Stretch Is to Step into the Game

We have met the enemy and he is us.

—Walt Kelly, Pogo[1]

The third stretch is the biggest: from the sidelines into the game. If we want to get important things done in complex situations, then we can't spend our time just watching and blaming and cajoling others. We have to step in.

In conventional collaboration, we focus on trying to change what other people are doing. These others may be people outside our collaboration who are the targets of our collective activities, or they may be fellow collaborators whose behavior we think ought to change. This approach works when we are in simple situations that are under control: when we can change what other people are doing. But when we are in complex, uncontrolled situations, we need to shift our focus onto what we ourselves are doing: how we are contributing to things being the way they are and what we need to do differently to change the way things are.

Stepping in means less distance and autonomy and more connection and conflict. It can feel thrilling and also terrifying.

"THEY NEED TO CHANGE!"

During 2005 and 2006, I was one of the leaders of an ambitious collaboration to reduce child malnutrition in India. The Bhavishya Alliance consisted of twenty-six organizations, including Indian government agencies, the United Nations Children's Fund, multinational and Indian corporations, and local nongovernmental and community organizations. These organizations assigned fifty-six members of their staff to work full-time in a "social laboratory" for eight weeks. This team's assignment was to cocreate a first set of innovative cross-organizational initiatives to reduce malnutrition. This initial effort set Bhavishya up for a successful six years of work on a series of initiatives that made a significant impact on malnutrition on India, and it became an important example of cross-sector collaboration.[2]

The biggest impact of Bhavishya on me, however, was from what was not successful during the first eight weeks.

The lab started off with high expectations and high pressure. The participating organizations had invested a lot to get this complicated project going. At one point, the complexity of what we were organizing overwhelmed me, and I turned for advice to Arun Maira, a businessman and public servant, and asked him what, really, we were trying to do. "You have to remember," he replied, "that most of the time when a group of stakeholder leaders get together to work on a problem, every one of them believes that if only the *other* ones would change what they are thinking and doing, then the problem would be solved. But if all the stakeholders are involved, then it can't all be the fault of others! The real innovation here is that we are inviting these leaders to reflect on how they might need to change what they themselves are doing."

As the deadline to deliver the initiatives approached and the stress increased, I began to worry that our design would not work, and my leadership contracted and hardened. I became more distant from the team, and my understanding of what was going on and my capacity to deal with it thoughtfully diminished. But I thought that if I held on more tightly to our plan and pushed harder, I could get the work over the goal line.

On the last day of our eight-week process, we held a meeting where we proposed four initiatives to the heads of the participating organizations (the bosses of the members of the lab team). We had worked hard and were exhausted but satisfied with where we had gotten to.

The bosses, however, saw things differently. Several of them were critical of our proposals and doubted that they were sound or viable. By the end of the day, almost none of our work had been approved. The team felt bewildered and distressed. I felt devastated.

The team spent three days debriefing this surprising and upsetting end of the lab. Everyone was disappointed and hurt. Many of them blamed me for what had gone wrong. More than ever before in my life, I felt humiliated and angry.

I left India and went home. Every single day for months, I stewed over how I had been mistreated and fantasized about how I would get revenge. I knew that I had made some mistakes and needed to change how I handled such situations, but I thought I was being victimized and that others needed to change too: that I shouldn't be expected to work on myself unless others were doing the same.

Then one day I came across a pamphlet written by the philosopher Martin Buber, which contained the following paragraph:

> This perspective, in which a man sees himself only as an individual contrasted with other individuals, and not as a genuine person whose transformation helps towards the transformation of the world, contains a fundamental error. The essential thing is to begin with oneself, and at this moment a man has nothing in the world to care about than this beginning. Any other attitude would distract him from what he is about to begin, weaken his initiative, and thus frustrate the entire bold undertaking.[3]

In reading this, I saw that I was making exactly this fundamental error: I was distracting myself from what I needed to do. It was not useful for me to focus on what those people I saw as my enemies should be doing: I needed to focus on what I should be doing differently to deal effectively with the challenges I was facing.

This is a pattern of behavior that I have often observed in myself and others. When we are faced with a challenging situation, we focus our attention first and foremost on what other people are doing or not doing or ought to be doing. As Maira said, our habitual thinking is that "*they* need to change!" The others we want to change may be far away or close by; they may be specific individuals or faceless populations; we may consider them friends or enemies. Humorist Jerome K. Jerome writes, "I like work: it fascinates me. I can sit and look at it for hours."[4] Blaming others is a common and lazy way to avoid doing our own work.

The question about collaborating that I am asked most frequently is, "How can we get them to . . . ?" This question betrays a hierarchical and black-and-white mind-set: us versus them, friends versus enemies, heroes versus villains, good versus bad, innocent versus guilty. But in nonhierarchical, noncontrolled, stretch collaboration, we cannot *get* anyone to do anything, so we need to take a different approach.

We blame and enemyfy others, both to defend and to define ourselves. We see ourselves self-centeredly as the protagonist at the center of the drama of what is going on around us, so when we experience a challenge, we react as if it is a personal attack against which we must defend ourselves. We are frightened of being hurt, so we separate and shield ourselves by asserting that we are right and the others are wrong. We fear that if we collaborate with those others, we will become contaminated or compromised—that we will betray what we stand for and who we are.

Philosopher René Girard says that we create enemies as a way to avoid dealing with conflict within our communities or within ourselves, as discussed in a piece in the *Raven Review*:

> We . . . control internal conflict by projecting our vio-
> lence outside the community onto a scapegoat. . . . The
> successful use of a scapegoat depends on the commu-
> nity's belief that they have found the cause and cure
> of their troubles in this "enemy." Once the enemy is
> destroyed or expelled, [the community experiences]
> a sense of relief and calm is restored. But the calm is
> temporary since the scapegoat was not really the cause
> or the cure of the conflict that led to his expulsion. . . .
> Too often our identity, and in particular our sense of
> our own goodness, is dependent on being . . . against
> someone or something else. . . . We need the other to be
> wicked to know we are good and whether or not they are
> actually wicked is beside the point.[5]

The problem with enemyfying is not that we never have enemies: we often face people and situations that present us with
difficulties and dangers. Moreover, any effort we make to effect
change in the world will create discomfort, resistance, and opposition. The real problem with enemyfying is that it distracts and
unbalances us. We cannot avoid others whom we find challenging, so we need to focus simply on deciding, given these challenges, what we ourselves will do next.

IF YOU'RE NOT PART OF THE PROBLEM, YOU CAN'T BE PART OF THE SOLUTION

There are two ways in which we can understand our relationship
to and role in a given situation. One way is to see our role as like
that of the director of a play who is instructing the actors on the
stage, or like that of a spectator who is watching the play. In both
of these cases we see ourselves as being apart from and outside of
the situation, and the situation as being created from above (by
the director). The actors are creators of the play, but the director
is the paramount leader or super-creator.

Two Ways to Relate to a Situation

You are a **director** or **spectator** of the
actors in the situation; you are *apart from*
(above or outside) it

You are **one of the cocreators** of the
situation; you are *a part of* (within) it

The other way to see our role is like that of an actor, or like a "spectactor" in the kind of play put on by Brazilian theater director Augusto Boal, where the audience also participates in and influences the action on the stage.[6] In these cases we see ourselves as part of and within the situation—as one of the participants in cocreating what is happening.

In stretch collaboration we are cocreators. And in this role we are able to make wise decisions about what to do to affect our situation only to the extent that we are able to balance ourselves.

We become unbalanced by overlooking ourselves: by focusing on what others, rather than ourselves, need to be doing. The boon we obtain by shifting our attention from the former to the latter is that we liberate ourselves and give ourselves agency: now we have a direct opportunity to effect change. Instead of blaming others and pushing or cajoling or waiting for them to do their work—which rarely succeeds—we can get on with our own.

Getting on with our own work requires us to see and acknowledge our own role and responsibility. Leadership scholar Bill Torbert once told me, "The old activist quip, 'If you're not part of the solution, you're part of the problem' actually misses a more important point, which is that if you are not part of the problem, then you cannot be part of the solution." Unless we can grasp how what we are doing is contributing to our situation, we will have no way to change that situation, except from above, by forcing.

Stretch collaboration therefore requires that we see ourselves as part of, rather than apart from, the situation we are trying to address. I can phone home to say that I will be late "because I am in traffic" or "because I am traffic." The latter explanation explicitly opens up my options to work with others to change the situation.

We also become unbalanced in the opposite way, by seeing ourselves as the center of the world. Self-centeredness means that we arrogantly overestimate the correctness and value of our own perspectives and actions, and we underestimate those of others.

This impedes collaboration because it distorts our understanding of the situation we are in and what we need to do, and it creates conflicts with the others we are discounting.

We contract self-centeredly when we are frightened of losing our position and identity. More than only being afraid of failing, we are afraid of *being* a failure. Moreover, many of our most cherished identities—expert, professional, authority, leader, hero—impede collaboration because they place us hierarchically above or apart from others. Collaborating with others, especially others who do not agree with or like or trust us, requires us to join with them, shoulder to shoulder, as peers and equals. It requires us, as Anja Koehne said, to abandon "feeling superior as a condition of being."

Arun Maira often reminded me of the pitfalls of self-centeredness. "You shouldn't take things so personally," he once chided me. "Things happen that you have to deal with, but it doesn't help for you to make them all about you." Another time, I asked him how we could know if the large-scale change work we were doing was having an impact. "Your wish to prove that you are making a difference is egotistical," he said. "Keep in mind the key sentence of the *Bhagavad Gita*: 'The work is yours, but not the fruits thereof.' "[7] This advice liberated me to do my work conscientiously but without taking on responsibility for outcomes I could not control.

BE A PIG RATHER THAN A CHICKEN

The essence of the third stretch is assuming responsibility for the role that we ourselves are playing in the situation we are trying to change, and therefore for what we need to do differently in order for the situation to change. This stretch is challenging because it requires us to take the risk of engaging fully in the situation and so being changed or hurt by it. It requires us to be willing to sacrifice some of what feels known, familiar, comfortable, and safe. "In a ham omelet," the quip goes, "the chicken is involved but the pig is committed." Stretch collaboration requires us to be pigs rather than merely chickens.

Fifteen years ago I a series of several workshops with a Paraguayan colleague, Jorge Talavera. My Spanish was not very good, and neither was his English, so our communication had to be brief and to the point. We became attentive to the moment in a workshop when the team's work would suddenly start to advance, which we called "el click." This click, we observed, was the moment when the team members saw, usually with surprise and often with consternation, that in order for the situation they were working on to change, they themselves—not only others— had to change.

I have noticed the impact of this click on my own work. When I am lazily blaming others for what is going on, I feel unhappy and helpless. But when I see and commit to what I can do about what is going on, I feel alert and energetic. This does not mean that I am always successful in affecting what is going on—but I am successful more often. The projects I have really thrown myself into (including Bhavishya and the others recounted in this book) have been the ones that have had the greatest impact and have taught me the most.

The essential practice required for stepping into the game is, then, to attend to ourselves. When we notice ourselves blaming others—focusing on what they are doing and what we hope or demand that they do differently—we need to bring our attention back to what we ourselves are doing and what we need to do differently. Sometimes what we need to do is to try to influence others—but now we are taking responsibility for, and willing to change, our part in the situation that we are all part of. Whenever we find ourselves distracted by others, we need to come back to the simple question, what must we do next?

Conclusion: How to
Learn to Stretch

*T*his book is a call both for more collective action and for more individual responsibility. It argues that increasingly, in all spheres—at home and work, on local and national and global issues—if we want to get things done, we need to collaborate, not only with colleagues and friends but also with opponents and enemies. And it argues that to be able to collaborate in such complex and conflictual and uncontrolled contexts, we need to stretch.

Up to now, this book has offered ideas about how to stretch. The purpose of this concluding chapter is to help you take these ideas and put them into practice.

Stretch collaboration is an unconventional way of working with others that involves three basic shifts:

The first stretch, embracing conflict and connection, requires you to employ two complementary drives rather than choosing only one: power, the drive to self-realization that is expressed in asserting; and love, the drive to reunification that is expressed in engaging. You need to employ these drives alternately rather than simultaneously.

The second stretch, experimenting a way forward, requires you to employ dialoguing and presencing, which enable new possibilities to emerge, rather than only downloading and debating, which reinforce the status quo. This means opening up your talking and especially your listening.

The third stretch, stepping into the game, requires you to plunge into the action, willing to change yourself, rather than remaining outside and above it, only trying to change other people.

Most people find these stretches unfamiliar and uncomfortable because they demand changing ingrained behaviors. The way to learn new behaviors is to practice them over and over. And the way to start practicing is to try out a few simple new actions, pay attention to what works and what doesn't, adjust and repeat, and build from there. This practicing requires acting with curiosity and openness: as in theatrical improvisation, to say yes and allow yourself to be changed by what then happens. It also requires unflinching self-reflectiveness in observing what you are doing and the impact you are having; enlist a colleague or friend who knows you well and is willing to help you by providing feedback.

Here is a six-week program of exercises you can do to begin to practice the three stretches.[1] You will need the following:

❑ A willingness to try out new actions

❑ A sense of humor

❑ A notebook and pen (or another way to take notes)

❑ A colleague or friend

These exercises are presented on the assumption that you will do them alone, with your colleague giving you feedback. Alternatively, you can do the exercises together with another person or a group, which would enable you to learn from their experiences as well.

A key practice in doing these exercises is taking time each day to write down your observations and reflections. This journaling can be in a notebook or on your phone or computer—whatever is easiest. What is crucial is that you take the time to reflect every day, since becoming consciously aware of your present behaviors is essential to creating new ones. Some people find it useful to write in a journal at the same time every day, say in the evening.

If you want to see the whole picture before you begin, you can read through all of the exercises before you start the first one. Or you can dive right into the first exercise and allow the whole picture to become clear as you go along.

WEEK 1: FIRST STRETCH
Establish a baseline for your use of power and love.

1. Consider all the time you spend collaborating (working with others), at home and at work and in the community. Estimate how much of this time you spend primarily employing power and asserting and only secondarily employing love and engaging, and how much you do the reverse (these two numbers should add up to 100 percent). Be honest in this self-assessment, which concerns how you are acting now, not how you wish you were acting.

   » *When you are working with others, what percentage of your time are you primarily employing power and asserting?*

   » *What percentage of your time are you primarily employing love and engaging?*

   » *Which of these two ways of acting feels most comfortable to you?*

   » *Is your use of these ways of acting different in different settings, for example, at home, at work, and in the community?*

2. Ask your colleague to write down his or her assessment of you by answering the above questions (and to do this before you share your self-assessment).

3. Meet with your colleague.

   » *Share your self-assessment.*

» *Listen to your colleague's assessment of you.*

» *Discuss the differences between these two assessments.*

» *Take notes.*

» *Agree on a time to talk again at the end of the week.*

4. For one week, observe your actions as you work with others. Take time each day to write down your observations and reflections.

5. At the end of the week, compare your observations with your and your colleague's initial assessments. Write down your insights.

6. Talk with your colleague and share your observations and insights. Ask for his or her feedback.

WEEK 2: FIRST STRETCH

Balance your use of power and love, not by weakening your stronger drive but by strengthening your weaker one.

1. List the actions you took during Week 1 that expressed your weaker side: the way of acting (either engaging or asserting) that you employed less and that felt less comfortable.

2. Choose three of these actions to practice this week. Your objective is to employ and strengthen your weaker side, especially when you feel you are at risk of overemploying your stronger one.

3. Tell your colleague the actions you will be practicing this week. Ask for his or her feedback.

4. For the rest of the week, while you are working with others, practice these three actions. Take time each day to write down your observations and reflections.

5. At the end of the week, talk with your colleague, and share your observations and insights. Ask for his or her feedback.

WEEK 3: SECOND STRETCH
Establish a baseline for how you are talking and listening.

1. Consider all the time you spend collaborating (working with others), at home and at work and in the community. Estimate how much of this time you spend employing each of the four ways of talking and listening (these four numbers should add up to 100 percent). Be honest in this self-assessment, which concerns how you are acting now, not how you wish you were acting.

   » *When you are working with others, what percentage of your time are you downloading: saying what is true or safe or polite, and not listening to others?*

   » *What percentage of your time are you debating: saying what you really think, and listening to judge what is correct?*

   » *What percentage of your time are you dialoguing: saying where you are coming from and listening to where others are coming from?*

   » *What percentage of your time are you presencing: saying and listening to what you perceive to be emerging in your situation as a whole?*

   » *Which of these ways of acting feels most comfortable to you? Which feels least comfortable?*

   » *Is your use of these ways of acting different in different settings—for example, at home, at work, and in your community?*

2. Ask your colleague to write down his or her assessment of you by answering the above questions (and to do this before you share your self-assessment).

3. Meet with your colleague.

   » *Share your self-assessment.*

   » *Listen to your colleague's assessment of you.*

» *Discuss the differences between these two assessments.*

» *Take notes.*

» *Agree on a time to talk again at the end of the week.*

4. For one week, when you are working with others, pay attention to how you are talking and listening. Do this by using the following precise sentence stubs. When you are downloading, start your sentences with the words "The truth is . . ." When you are debating, start with "In my opinion . . ." When you are dialoguing, start with "In my experience . . ." And when you are presencing, start with "What I am noticing here and now is . . ." Take time each day to write down your observations and reflections.

5. At the end of the week, compare your observations with your and your colleague's initial assessments. Write down your insights.

6. Talk with your colleague and share your observations and insights. Ask for his or her feedback.

WEEK 4: SECOND STRETCH
Shift your talking and listening away from downloading and debating toward dialoguing and presencing.

1. For one week, while you are working with others, employ only dialoguing and presencing. When you notice yourself downloading or debating, shift to dialoguing ("In my experience . . .") or presencing ("What I am noticing here and now is . . ."). Take time each day to write down your observations and reflections.

2. At the end of the week, talk with your colleague and share your observations and insights. Ask for his or her feedback.

WEEKS 5 AND 6: THIRD STRETCH
Step from the sidelines into the game.

1. Think of a collaborative project or initiative (at home or at work or in the community) that you are involved in and that seems stuck.

2. Write out descriptions of what is going on in this project from two different perspectives:

   » *The first description is as if you are observing or directing this situation from the outside. Describe in detail what other people are doing that is contributing to the situation being as it is now, and what they need to do differently to enable the situation to get unstuck and move forward.*

   » *The second description is as if you are participating in and cocreating this situation from the inside. Describe in detail what you are doing that is contributing to the situation being as it is now, and what you need to do differently to enable the situation to get unstuck and move forward.*

3. Now list all of the actions, large and small, that you are currently taking that relate to this project. Go through this list and decide, for each action, whether you are taking it primarily from the first perspective (as an observer or director) or primarily from the second (as a participant and cocreator).

4. Share your two descriptions and your list of actions with your colleague. Ask for his or her feedback. What does he or she think is clear and insightful? What does he or she think might be inaccurate or missing?

5. Choose two actions from your list that arise from the first perspective (as an observer or director). Decide, for each action, whether you will abandon it (stop doing it without replacing it) or adapt it (so that it still fulfills its function), in order to strengthen your role as a cocreator.

6. Choose another action from your list that arises from the second perspective (as a cocreator). Decide how you can strengthen it, in order to strengthen your role as a cocreator.

7. Over the next two weeks, implement these three changes to your actions. Take time each day to write down your observations and reflections.

8. At the end of each week, talk with your colleague and share your observations and insights. Ask for his or her feedback.

THE WAY FORWARD

As you practice these new behaviors for a while and become more comfortable with them, you can try them out in more complex and conflictual situations. Sometimes your actions will produce the results you intend, and sometimes they won't. Your goal is not to collaborate impeccably—in such a social endeavor, this would not be possible—but to become more aware of what you are doing and the impact you are having, and to be able to adapt and learn more quickly. This is how you will move from unconscious incompetence to conscious incompetence to conscious competence to unconscious competence.

The primary obstacle you will face in learning to stretch is overcoming the familiarity and comfort of your habitual way of doing things. You will need to move away from a declarative "It must be this way" toward a subjunctive "It could be this way." You will need to loosen your attachment to your own opinions, positions, and identities: to sacrifice your smaller, constricted self to your larger, freer one. These stretches can therefore feel both frightening and liberating.

Tai chi teacher Wolfe Lowenthal says this about the martial art of push hands:

No matter how hard and unyielding your opponent, our inability to deal gently with him is indicative of our own stuckness. It is the exploration and eventual dissolving of the stuckness—not winning—that is the point of push hands. The "game" we really should be playing is with ourselves; we are coming face to face with the physical expression of the issues we hide from in our lives. In this confrontation with the self there lies the possibility of progress. We thank our opponent for providing us with this opportunity.[2]

So in learning to collaborate, the people you think of as your enemies can, surprisingly, play a helpful role. Stretching requires you to move toward rather than away from different others. You will learn the most in those situations you find most difficult: when others do not do as you want them to and so force you to pause and find a fresh way forward.

Your enemies can be your greatest teachers.

Notes

All of the quotes in this book that are not noted here are from personal communications.

Chapter 1: Collaboration Is Becoming More Necessary and More Difficult

1. Lewis Thomas, "On the Uncertainty of Science," *Key Reporter*, Autumn 1980, 10.

2. Ana Marie Cox, "Aasif Mandvi Knows How to Make America Great Again," *New York Times*, October 4, 2016.

3. Quoted in Walter Winchell, "Walter Winchell On Broadway," *Laredo Times*, November 9, 1949.

4. *The Concise Oxford Dictionary of Current English* (Oxford: Oxford University Press, 1983).

Chapter 2: Collaboration Is Not the Only Option

1. James Gimian and Barry Boyce, *The Rules of Victory: How to Transform Chaos and Conflict—Strategies from* The Art of War (Boston: Shambhala, 2008), 11.

2. See Adam Kahane, *Transformative Scenario Planning: Working Together to Change the Future* (San Francisco: Berrett-Koehler Publishers, 2012), 1–13.

3. See Hal Hamilton, "System Leaders for Sustainable Food," *Stanford Social Innovation Review*, Winter 2015, and www.sustainablefoodlab.org.

Chapter 3: Conventional, Constricted Collaboration Is Becoming Obsolete

1. John Maynard Keynes, *The General Theory of Employment, Interest, and Money* (New York: Harcourt, Brace & World, 1965), vii.

2. Kees van der Heijden, *Scenarios: The Art of Strategic Conversation* (Chichester, West Sussex, England: John Wiley & Sons, 1996), 21.

3. Horst W. J. Rittel and Melvin M. Webber, "Dilemmas in a General Theory of Planning," *Policy Sciences* 4 (1973), 155.

4. Graham Leicester and Maureen O'Hara, *Ten Things to Do in a Conceptual Emergency* (Fife, Scotland: International Futures Forum, 2003), 5.

5. Isaiah Berlin, "A Message to the 21st Century," *New York Review of Books*, October 23, 2014.

6. Michael Fulwiler, "Managing Conflict: Solvable vs. Perpetual Problems," http://www.gottman.com, July 2, 2012.

CHAPTER 4: Unconventional, Stretch Collaboration Is Becoming Essential

1. André Gide, *The Counterfeiters* (New York: Vintage Books, 1973), 353.

2. Juan Manuel Santos, "Presentacíon" ("Presentation"), in Adam Kahane, *Poder y Amor: Teoría y Práctica para el Cambio Social* ("Power and Love: A Theory and Practice of Social Change") (La Paz, Bolivia: Plural, 2011), 14.

3. *Transformative Scenario Planning*, 79–90.

4. "Siempre en búsqueda de la paz" ("Always Searching for Peace"), October 7, 2016, es.presidencia.gov.co.

CHAPTER 5: The First Stretch Is to Embrace Conflict and Connection

1. Leonard Cohen, "Different Sides," *Old Ideas*, 2012.

2. See Elena Díez Pinto et al., *Los Escenarios del Futuro* ("Scenarios of the Future") (Guatemala City, Guatemala: Visión Guatemala, 1999); and Elena Díez Pinto, "Building Bridges of Trust: Visión Guatemala, 1998–2000," in Katrin Käufer et al., *Learning Histories: Democratic Dialogue Regional Project*, Working Paper 3 (New York: United Nations Development Programme Regional Bureau for Latin America

and the Caribbean, 2004). See also Adam Kahane, *Power and Love: A Theory and Practice of Social Change* (San Francisco: Berrett-Koehler Publishers, 2009), 32–35, 42–46, 113–27.

3. Elena Díez Pinto, "Building Bridges of Trust," 30.

4. David Suzuki, "Imagining a Sustainable Future: Foresight over Hindsight," Jack Beale Lecture on the Global Environment, University of New South Wales, September 21, 2013.

5. Arthur Koestler, *The Ghost in the Machine* (London: Hutchinson & Co, 1967), 48.

6. Adam Kahane, ed., *Possible Canadas: Perspectives on Our Pasts, Presents, and Futures*, project report, 2015.

7. See *Power and Love*, 2; and Paul Tillich, *Love, Power, and Justice: Ontological Analyses and Ethical Applications* (New York: Oxford University Press, 1954), 25, 36.

8. Barry Oshry, "Power Without Love and Love Without Power: A Systems Perspective" (unpublished paper, 2009).

9. Martin Luther King Jr., "Where Do We Go from Here?" Speech to the Southern Christian Leadership Conference, Atlanta, Georgia, August 16, 1967.

10. Robert Caro, *Master of the Senate: The Years of Lyndon Johnson* (New York: Vintage, 2003, reprint ed.), 834.

11. See Barry Johnson, *Polarity Management: Identifying and Managing Unsolvable Problems* (Amherst, MA: HRD Press, 2014).

12. James Hillman, *Kinds of Power: A Guide to Its Intelligent Uses* (New York: Doubleday, 1995), 108.

13. This evolutionary process is explained by the different but related cycle described by ecologist C. S. Holling in his writing about systemic resiliency. In this cycle, periods of stable and predictable growth and consolidation are interrupted by shorter periods of destabilizing and unpredictable innovation and reorganization. C. S. Holling, "Understanding the Complexity of Economic, Ecological, and Social Systems Ecosystems," *Ecosystems* 4, issue 5 (August 2001), 390–405.

CHAPTER 6: The Second Stretch Is to Experiment a Way Forward

1. "Caminante, no hay camino, se hace camino al andar." In Antonio Machado, "Proverbios y cantares XXIX," *Campos de Castilla* (Madrid: Editorial Poesia eres tu, 2006), 131.

2. "The War on Drugs: Are we paying too high a price?" Count the Costs, 2013, http://www.countthecosts.org/sites/default/files/War%20on%20Drugs%20-%20Count%20the%20Costs%207%20cost%20summary.pdf, 3.

3. Juan Manuel Santos, "Consumer countries should take more effective measures to reduce the demand for illicit drugs," November 22, 2011, presidencia.gov.co.

4. *Scenarios for the Drug Problem in the Americas 2013–2025* (Washington, DC: Organization of American States, 2013).

5. Juan Manuel Santos, "Declaración del Presidente Juan Manuel Santos después de recibir el informe 'El problema de las drogas en las Américas' por parte de la Organización de Estados Americanos" ("Speech given by President Juan Manuel Santos on receiving the report 'The Drug Problem in the Americas' by the Organization of American States"), May 17, 2013, es.presidencia.gov.co.

6. José Miguel Insulza, "The OAS drug report: 16 months of debates and consensus" (Washington, DC: Organization of American States, 2014), 3.

7. Peter Senge et al., *The Dance of Change: The Challenges to Sustaining Momentum in a Learning Organization* (New York: Crown Business, 1999).

8. Quoted in Barbara Heinzen, *Feeling for Stones: Learning and Invention When Facing the Unknown* (London: Barbara Heinzen, 2006).

9. Karl E. Weick, *Making Sense of the Organization* (Oxford: Blackwell Publishing, 2001), 345–46.

10. Henry Mintzberg and James A. Waters, "Of Strategies, Deliberate and Emergent," *Strategic Management Journal* 6, no. 3 (1985), 257.

11. Henri-Georges Clouzot, *The Mystery of Picasso*, film, 1956.

12. C. Otto Scharmer, *Theory U: Leading from the Future as It Emerges* (San Francisco: Berrett-Koehler Publishers, 2009).

13. John Keats, *The Complete Poetical Works and Letters of John Keats* (Boston: Houghton, Mifflin and Company, 1899), 277.

14 Shunryu Suzuki, *Zen Mind, Beginner's Mind* (Boston: Shambhala, 2011), 1.

15. Katrin Käufer, "Learning from the Civic Scenario Project: A Tool for Facilitating Social Change?" in Käufer et al., *Learning Histories*.

16. Scharmer, *Theory U*, 267.

17. Peter Senge, Otto Scharmer, Joseph Jaworski, and Betty Sue Flowers, *Presence: Human Purpose and the Field of the Future* (New York: Broadway Business, 2008).

Chapter 7: The Third Stretch Is to Step into the Game

1. Wikipedia, "Pogo (comic strip)," https://wikipedia.org/wiki/Pogo_(comic_strip).

2. See "The Bhavishya Alliance: Legacy and Learning from an Indian Multi-sector Partnership to Reduce Child Undernutrition," project report, April 2012; Kahane, *Power and Love*; and Zaid Hassan, *The Social Labs Revolution: A New Approach to Solving Our Most Complex Challenges* (San Francisco: Berrett-Koehler Publishers, 2014).

3. Martin Buber, *The Way of Man: According to the Teaching of Hasidism* (Wallingford, PA: Pendle Hill Publications, 1960), 21.

4. Jerome K. Jerome, *Three Men in a Boat* (London: Penguin, 2008), 49.

5. "An Introduction to Mimetic Theory" and "Scapegoating," *Raven Review*, https://www.ravenfoundation.org/faqs/.

6. Augusto Boal, *Theatre of the Oppressed* (New York: Theatre Communications Group, 1993).

7. Eknath Easwaran, trans., *The Bhagavad Gita* (Tomales, CA: Nilgiri Press, 1998), chapter 2, verse 47.

Conclusion: How to Learn to Stretch

1. These exercises were developed by my colleague Ian Prinsloo, with input and testing by Lucilene Danciguer, Nicole Endicott, Karin Hommels, Anaí Linares Méndez, Mariana Miranda, Elizabeth

Pinnington, Monica Pohlmann, Manuela Restrepo, and Mahmood Sonday.

2. Wolfe Lowenthal, *There Are No Secrets: Professor Cheng Man-ch'ing and His Tai Chi Chuan* (Berkeley: North Atlantic Books, 1991), 19.

Acknowledgments

*W*orking on this book has been a wonderful experience of generative and generous collaboration. This book has grown out of my experiences of working alongside colleagues on challenging projects that we thought mattered. For this companionship on the projects recounted in this book, I am grateful to Steve Atkinson, Brenna Atnikov, Adam Blackwell, Mille Bojer, Manuel José Carvajal, Sumit Champrasit, Elena Díez Pinto, Betty Sue Flowers, Rossana Fuentes Berain, Oscar Grossmann, Hal Hamilton, Zaid Hassan, Stephen Huddart, Joseph Jaworski, Goft Kanyaporn, Ruth Krivoy, Pieter le Roux, Aeumporn Loipradit, Julio Madrazo, Vincent Maphai, Joe McCarron, Anaí Linares Méndez, Joaquin Moreno, Juan Carlos Morris, Gustavo Mutis, Reola Phelps, Elizabeth Pinnington, Monica Pohlmann, Ian Prinsloo, Tom Rautenberg, Manuela Restrepo, Surita Sandosham, Adalberto Saviñon Diez de Sollano, Valeria Scorza, Paul Simons, and Jorge Talavera.

In writing this book, I experimented with a process (supported by Mitch Anthony and Tiê Franco Brotto) of "writing out loud": publishing online one draft chapter at a time and requesting feedback from interested readers. The response of readers was overwhelmingly enthusiastic and helpful, and I am grateful for the thoughtful input (through this and other channels) from Chris Abeles, Michel Adam, Chris Altmikus, Charles Anosike, Antonio Aranibar, Helen Astarte, Steve Atkinson, Jeff Barnum, Antonia Baum, Herman Bavinck, Sabina Berman, Duan Biggs, Rick Black, Peter Block, Mille Bojer, Mark Burdon, Mark Cabaj, Doug Canterbury-Counts, Julia Canty, Anne Weber Carlsen, Jose Bucci Casari, Jean Pierre Chabot, Sumit

Champrasit, Michael Chender, Tom Christensen, Miljenko Cimeša, David Cooper, Chris Corrigan, Marie-Claire Dagher, James Davis, Milton Dawes, David Diamond, Hein Dijksterhuis, Hugo Diogo, Debra Dunn, Col Duthie, Martín Echavarria, Dawn Ellison, Nicole Endacott, Caroline Figueres, Betty Sue Flowers, Rebecca Freeth, Katherine Fulton, Hermann Funk, Deb Dugan Garcia, Victor Garcia, Robert Gass, Michel Gelobter, James Gimian, Stacie Goffin, Pierre Goirand, Danny Graham, John Griffin, Oscar Grossmann, Vinay Gunther, Wietske Hagg, Nancy Hale, Patricia Hale, Saleena Han, Eiji Harada, Cesar De Hart, Martin Hawkes, Cressida Heyes, Allison Hewlitt, Daniel Hirschler, Jon Hoel, Stephen Huddart, Monique Janmaat, Barry Johnson, Brad Johnston, Al Jones, David Kahane, Dorothy Kahane, Jed Kahane, Goft Kanyaporn, Alla Kholina, Sharon Joy Kleitsch, Barbara Kruse, S. Kulshrestha, Sean Lafleur, Lorenzo Lara, Dan Leahy, Graham Leicester, Meg Levie, Kathy Lewis, Maria Lewytzky-Milligan, Charles Lines, Ralf Lippold, Katharina Lobeck, Aeumporn Loipradit, Janine Machet, Robbie Macpherson, Colleen Magner, Arun Maira, Amy Marks, Sandra Martinez, Joe McCarron, Ceasar McDowell, Bill McIntosh, Jeanne McPherson, Tim Merry, Denny Minno, Colin Mitchell, Eileen Moir, Tina Monberg, Carol Moore, Arthur Muliro, Anant Nadkarni, Jerry Nagel, Jo Nelson, Maria Ana Neves, James Newcomb, Bangani Ngeleza, Terry Nichols, Jos Niesten, Batian Nieuwerth, Sibout Nooteboom, Barbara Nussbaum, Riichiro Oda, Daniel Olding, Barry Oshry, Hervé Ott, Wendy Palmer, Scott Perret, Reola Phelps, Gifford Pinchot, Elizabeth Pinnington, Monica Pohlmann, David Portillo, Anthony Prangley, Ian Prinsloo, Melissa Josephine Ramos, Martin Rausch, Deborah Ravetz, Jerome Ravetz, Mark Ritchie, Marti Roach, Alain Ruche, Christel Scholten, Henry Senko, David Shandler, Gary Shunk, Liz Skelton, Dylan Skybrook, Timothy Smith, Dirk Steen, Don de Souza, Uta Stolz, Kim Stryker, Jill Swenson, Susan Szpakowski, James Taylor, Yvonne Thackray, Theodore Thomas, David Thompson, Ralph Torrie, Alper Utku, Marco Valente,

Karen Verburgh, Pablo Villoch, Pierre Vuarin, Adrian Wagner, Colleen Walker, Pascal Wattiaux, Doug Weinfield, Victoria Wilding, Sue Wittenoom, Heidi De Wolf, Kerry Woodcock, Teresa Woodland, Bertram Zichel, and Rosa Zubizarreta.

The expression of the ideas in this book has been enriched enormously through conversations with my longtime collaborator Jeff Barnum, who also created the beautiful illustrations.

This book offers not just a theory but also a practice of collaborating, and in parallel with writing the text, I have created a suite of capacity-building exercises, seminars, and workshops. My great partner in this effort has been my colleague Ian Prinsloo.

One of the best parts of my experience as an author has been working with the outstanding professional team at Berrett-Koehler. My thanks in particular to Michael Crowley, Paula Durbin-Westby, Karen Hill Green, Linda Jupiter, Laura Lind, Elissa Rabellino, Jeevan Sivasubramaniam, Edward Wade, Lasell Whipple, and especially Steve Piersanti.

I would not be able to do this work without the encouragement and comradeship of my long-standing friends in Reos Partners, in particular the members of our Global Leadership Team: Steve Atkinson, Mille Bojer, Leigh Gassner, John Griffin, Colleen Magner, Batian Nieuwerth, Jos Niesten, Elizabeth Pinnington, Monica Pohlmann, Christel Scholten, and especially Joe McCarron.

I apologize to anyone whose contribution I have failed to acknowledge. The remaining faults of the book are, of course, my own.

My greatest debt is to Dorothy, for all that she does and is.

Index

Page locators in italics indicate illustrations

About the Author

*A*dam Kahane has always wanted to work on important and difficult challenges. When he was younger,
he thought of these challenges as problems that could be solved
by experts, and he wanted to be one. He studied physics at
McGill University in Montreal and energy and resource economics at the University of California, Berkeley, and held a series
of public policy research positions in North America, Europe,
and Japan. Then he worked as a corporate planner at Pacific Gas
and Electric Company in San Francisco and as the head of global
social, political, economic, environmental, and technological
scenarios at Royal Dutch Shell in London.

Adam's thinking about how to approach difficult challenges
changed dramatically in 1991, when he helped a team of South
African leaders think through how to effect the transition from
apartheid to democracy. He learned that such complex matters
are not simply problems to be solved by experts but problematic
situations to be worked through by
stakeholders. He also learned that
diverse teams—made up not just
of colleagues and friends but also
of opponents and enemies—can do
this work collaboratively.

This experience transformed
Adam's understanding of his voca-
tion. He left Shell, moved to Cape
Town, and threw himself into sup-
Source: Móric van der Meer   porting collaborative efforts to

address complex challenges. He cofounded Reos Partners, a social enterprise that guides such efforts around the world.

Over the last twenty-five years, Adam has worked in this way in more than fifty countries, with executives and politicians, generals and guerrillas, civil servants and trade unionists, community activists and clergy. Along the way he learned that collaboration is not as straightforward as he thought it was, and that this is true not only for extraordinary multistakeholder collaborations but also for ordinary ones at work and at home.

Adam is a director of Reos Partners, where his consulting, facilitating, and teaching all focus on helping people work together to address their most important and difficult challenges. He and his wife, Dorothy, have four children and nine grandchildren and live in Cape Town and Montreal.

www.adamkahane.com

About Reos Partners

How can we work together to solve the problems we have created?

Reos Partners is an international social enterprise that knows how to make real progress.

We've been designing and facilitating systemic change projects for twenty years and have built up a rigorous set of transformative methods for addressing complex, stuck challenges.

Using a pragmatic and creative approach, we partner with governments, corporations, and civil society organizations on humanity's most crucial issues: education, health, food, energy, the environment, development, justice, security, and peace. Again and again, we enable people mired in complexity, confusion, and conflict to work together to construct new realities— and a better future.

We help you challenge the status quo, together

The starting point for progress is a diverse coalition that is ready to challenge the status quo. Every Reos Partners project brings together stakeholders from across a whole system. Politicians, activists, executives, generals, guerrillas, unionists, activists, artists, researchers, clergy, community leaders . . . Diversity may feel like the problem, but it is at the heart of problem solving. Working as guides, we skillfully engage people with different perspectives and interests to collaborate on shared concerns.

Proven methods for systemic change

Reos Partners projects occur at three scales: events of a few days, processes of several months, and platforms that operate for years. A single event can spark new insights, relationships, and capacities, while a long-term platform can enable new experiments, initiatives, and movements—and, ultimately, systemic transformation.

We take a custom approach to every situation, but we often employ at least one of four tested methods: dialogue interviews, learning journeys, transformative scenarios, and social labs. We also offer training and coaching to build the capacities and skills that enable enduring systems change.

Real progress on vital challenges, worldwide

We've learned that there is no quick fix: systemic change takes time, energy, resources, and skill. But with these in place, our most successful projects take on lives of their own, spawning resilient networks, alliances, and ecologies.

Let's work together

We operate both globally and locally, with offices in Cambridge (Massachusetts), Geneva, Johannesburg, Melbourne, Montreal, São Paulo, and The Hague. Visit us at www.reospartners.com/ stretchcollaboration.

A Note from the Artist,
Jeff Barnum

I am grateful to Adam for our many collaborations over the years, including this latest project, the artwork for this book. I find our collaboration remarkable because he and I are so very different. We see the world differently; we have different priorities, different experiences, and different life goals. But what should divide us we choose to see as complementary.

In 2007, we and other colleagues cofounded Reos Partners and started working together around the world. As we supported leaders facing complex, seemingly insurmountable challenges, I repeatedly found myself teaching them about creativity, self-transformation, and other "inner" aspects of rising to the enormous task of changing paradigms and systems. At the same time, another set of questions arose for me. How is healthy soci-

ety possible? If you study great art, you can get a sense of what makes it great, but what about creating social realities? Is it possible, and what is required, for many individuals to cocreate healthier, more functional societies?

I left Reos in 2014 to focus on these questions full time with Magenta Studios (www.magenta.fm).

Also by Adam Kahane

Transformative Scenario Planning
Working Together to Change the Future

People who are trying to solve tough economic, social, and environmental problems often find themselves frustratingly stuck. They can't solve their problems in their current context, which is too unstable or unfair or unsustainable. They can't transform this context on their own—it's too complex to be grasped or shifted by any one person or organization or sector. Transformative scenario planning is a powerful new methodology for dealing with these challenges. It enables us to transform ourselves and our relationships and thereby the systems of which we are a part. At a time when divisions within and among societies are producing so much stuckness and suffering, it offers hope—and a proven approach—for moving forward together.

Paperback, 168 pages, ISBN 978-1-60994-490-2
PDF ebook ISBN 978-1-60994-491-9
ePub ebook ISBN 978-1-60994-492-6
Digital audio ISBN 978-1-62656-018-5

Berrett–Koehler Publishers, Inc.
www.bkconnection.com

800.929.2929

Power and Love
A Theory and Practice of Social Change

The two methods frequently employed to solve our toughest social problems—either violence and aggression or endless negotiation and compromise—are fundamentally flawed. This is because the seemingly contradictory drives behind these approaches—*power*, the desire to achieve one's purpose, and *love*, the urge to unite with others—are actually complementary. As Dr. Martin Luther King Jr. put it, "Power without love is reckless and abusive, and love without power is sentimental and anemic."

Adam Kahane delves deeply into the dual natures of both power and love and relates how, through trial and error, he has learned to balance them, offering practical guidance for how others can learn that balance as well.

Paperback, 192 pages, ISBN 978-1-60509-304-8
PDF ebook, ISBN 978-1-60509-305-5
ePub ebook ISBN 978-1-60509-653-7
Digital audio ISBN 978-1-62656-017-8

BK Berrett–Koehler Publishers, Inc.
www.bkconnection.com   **800.929.2929**

Solving Tough Problems
An Open Way of Talking, Listening, and Creating New Realities

"This breakthrough book addresses the central challenge of our time: finding a way to work together to solve the problems we have created."

—Nelson Mandela

Adam Kahane has worked on some of the most difficult problems in the world, from post-apartheid South Africa to Colombia during the civil war, Guatemala after the genocide, Israel-Palestine, Northern Ireland, Cyprus, and the Basque Country. Through these experiences, he has learned how to create environments that enable innovative new ideas and solutions to emerge and be implemented even in the most challenging contexts. Here Kahane tells his stories and distills from them an approach that all of us can use to solve our own toughest problems.

Paperback, 168 pages, ISBN 978-1-57675-464-1
PDF ebook, ISBN 978-1-57675-537-2
ePub ebook ISBN 978-1-60509-897-5

BK Berrett–Koehler Publishers, Inc.
www.bkconnection.com   800.929.2929

Berrett–Koehler
BK Publishers

Berrett-Koehler is an independent publisher dedicated to an ambitious mission: *Connecting people and ideas to create a world that works for all.*

We believe that the solutions to the world's problems will come from all of us, working at all levels: in our organizations, in our society, and in our own lives. Our BK Business books help people make their organizations more humane, democratic, diverse, and effective (we don't think there's any contradiction there). Our BK Currents books offer pathways to creating a more just, equitable, and sustainable society. Our BK Life books help people create positive change in their lives and align their personal practices with their aspirations for a better world.

All of our books are designed to bring people seeking positive change together around the ideas that empower them to see and shape the world in a new way.

And we strive to practice what we preach. At the core of our approach is Stewardship, a deep sense of responsibility to administer the company for the benefit of all of our stakeholder groups including authors, customers, employees, investors, service providers, and the communities and environment around us. Everything we do is built around this and our other key values of quality, partnership, inclusion, and sustainability.

This is why we are both a B-Corporation and a California Benefit Corporation—a certification and a for-profit legal status that require us to adhere to the highest standards for corporate, social, and environmental performance.

We are grateful to our readers, authors, and other friends of the company who consider themselves to be part of the BK Community. We hope that you, too, will join us in our mission.

A BK Business Book

We hope you enjoy this BK Business book. BK Business books pioneer new leadership and management practices and socially responsible approaches to business. They are designed to provide you with groundbreaking and practical tools to transform your work and organizations while upholding the triple bottom line of people, planet, and profits. High-five!

To find out more, visit **www.bkconnection.com**.

Berrett–Koehler
Publishers

Connecting people and ideas
to create a world that works for all

Dear Reader,

Thank you for picking up this book and joining our worldwide community of Berrett-Koehler readers. We share ideas that bring positive change into people's lives, organizations, and society.

To welcome you, we'd like to offer you a free e-book. You can pick from among twelve of our bestselling books by entering the promotional code **BKP92E** here: http://www.bkconnection.com/welcome.

When you claim your free e-book, we'll also send you a copy of our e-newsletter, the *BK Communiqué*. Although you're free to unsubscribe, there are many benefits to sticking around. In every issue of our newsletter you'll find

- A free e-book
- Tips from famous authors
- Discounts on spotlight titles
- Hilarious insider publishing news
- A chance to win a prize for answering a riddle

Best of all, our readers tell us, "Your newsletter is the only one I actually read." So claim your gift today, and please stay in touch!

Sincerely,

Charlotte Ashlock
Steward of the BK Website

Questions? Comments? Contact me at bkcommunity@bkpub.com.